3558

TWO HEARTS
ARE BETTER THAN
ONE

By the same author:

**OPEN HEART
THERAPY**

Robert Steven Mandel

TWO HEARTS ARE BETTER THAN ONE

Celestial Arts
Berkeley, California

Celestial Arts
P.O. Box 7327
Berkeley, California 94707

Library of Congress Cataloging-in-Publication Data

Mandel, Bob, 1943-
    Two hearts are better than one.

    Includes index.
        1.   Marriage—United States—Case studies.
2.   Married   people—United   States—Psychology—Case
studies.   3.   Interpersonal relations—Case studies.
I.   Title.
HQ734.M266   1986   306.8'1   85-29922
ISBN 0-89087-454-9

Cover Art by Eddie Kunze
Cover and Interior Design by Ken Scott
Typography by HMS Typography, Inc.

First Printing 1986
Made in the United States of America

10 9 8 7 6 5 4 3 2 1 — 92 91 90 89 88 87 86

I dedicate this book to Larry Block, whose writing and whose love, support, and *Write For Your Life* seminar have been such enormous inspirations to me . . .

To Larry and Lynne Block . . .

And to all those on the path towards perfect partnership.

CONTENTS

Foreword   1
Preface   3
Part One: Two Hearts Are Better Than One   6
    Love At First Fright   7
    End Of The Runway   14
    Broken Glasses   24
    24 Hours A Day   34
    Getting In Bed With Mom And Dad   50
    Three Is A Charm   62
    Put Your Money Where Your Heart Is 78
    Chosen Children   94
    Divine Comedy   106
    Two Hearts Are Better Than One   116
Part Two: Create-A-Mate   118
Part Three: Conscious Couples   152

FOREWORD

This book has three parts. Part One is the story of my relationship with my wife Mallie, the path we took, the lessons we learned and the conclusions we drew. The story is intended as an inspiration to all ''romantic realists,'' those of you seeking perfect partnership in the real world.

Part Two is the how-to-do-it part of the book. ''Create-a-Mate: how to attract and sustain your perfect loving relationship!'' is a proven system for creating conscious relationships and growing within yourself as you grow with your perfect partner.

Part Three is a tribute to other conscious couples.

When Mallie and I first met, we were very cynical about relationships. The only couples we had ever observed were involved either in long, tedious struggles or short, sweet, passionate affairs. We had had our share of both, and desired neither. So we chose to use our relationship as a place to experiment with the possibility of having an eternally sweet, passionate romance. Since we had no role models to follow, and since most of our friends were even more cynical than we were—in action, if not in word—we decided to make it our goal to create an abundance of wonderful, happy, prosperous, and spiritually conscious couples around us. We succeeded.

This book is a continuation of that goal. May you all experience the perfect love you so richly deserve!

PREFACE

"I can't wait to get my hands on you," Mallie said.
"Me, too," I replied.
"Good night, sweetheart."
"Good night."

I hung up the phone and rolled over. My bed was in Atlanta, Mallie's in New York. I was on the road leading a Loving Relationships Training. Mallie was home, minding the children. It was one of those rare weekends when we were not together. We felt totally together, tending different functions in our joint purpose, but at the same time we missed each other terribly. How odd, I was thinking as I closed my eyes. I remembered when the last thing on earth I wanted was to be with one woman twenty-four hours a day. And now here I was, bothered by a three day interruption of total togetherness. How far I must have come!

I took a deep breath and let it go, and tried to imagine Mallie rolling over in our bed back home. It was Sunday night. I would see her the next afternoon. I couldn't wait to get my hands on her. I drifted into a dream.

"Just wait till I get my hands on you!" my mother was screaming, chasing me around the kitchen table, a wooden hanger raised above her head. I could tell she meant business.

I ran into the bedroom, slamming the door behind me. I must have been twelve years old. I pushed my full weight against the door as my mother tried to open it.

"Open up!" she screamed. "Just wait till your father gets his hands on you!" She stormed off. I sat down on my bed and immediately dissolved into a puddle of tears. I knew I had done something horribly wrong, but I couldn't, for the life of me, figure out what. If my mother was this upset, I obviously had committed some terrible felony punishable only by some serious guilt. I was doing my part as best I could.

I lay down on the bed and closed my eyes. Why did everyone want to get their hands on me? I thought. And why did it always sound like punishment when people threatened to touch me? As a child I could get all the hugging and holding I needed at the simple drop of a tear. Now that I was twelve, all that had changed.

It seemed like the only time my parents wanted to touch me any more was when they wanted to hit me—which, in fact, they rarely did. I began to dream of a girl, one who would love me, hug me, and hold me as I craved to be held, one I could hold in total innocence forever. I could see her in a field. She seemed to be running away from me. I took off after her. She was blonde and swift, and I wanted to catch her more than anything in the world. The faster I ran, the more distance she seemed to put between us. It was hopeless. Finally, I collapsed in exhaustion. I looked up and she was standing above me.

"Whenever you stop running, I'll be here," she said.

"I stopped," I reminded her.

"I mean, for good," she said, smiling—as though she knew something it would take me years to find out.

I reached out for her, and then I woke up. My mother was knocking on the bedroom door.

"Open up!" she demanded. I jumped out of bed. "I want to talk to you."

I opened the door. I immediately regretted my decision when I looked into my mother's eyes. I could see how hurt she was, and I was ready to submit to the appropriate torture.

We sat down on the bed next to each other. She wasn't

angry as I'd expected her to be. She seemed resigned to some decision she had already made. For the first time I noticed she held a letter in her hand. It looked familiar.

"Who wrote you this letter?" She asked, waving it at me.

"Uhh . . ." I couldn't answer.

"It says," and she read it, " 'I love you and will never leave you. . . . Mallie!' What's a Mallie?"

"Oh, Mallie," I said. "You're going to love her. Just wait till you meet her.

"Who is she?"

"I don't know."

"She loves you and she'll never leave you and you don't know?"

"Not exactly. I haven't met her yet."

Suddenly I woke up in my bed in Atlanta. I was sweating and breathing hard. I wanted to hold Mallie in my arms forever. Someone was singing a song in my mind:

Bright are the stars that shine,
Dark is the sky;
I know this love of mine
Will never die . . .
And I love her . . .

P ♥ A ♥ R ♥ T

1

TWO HEARTS ARE BETTER THAN ONE

LOVE AT FIRST FRIGHT

"Do you want to stay the night?"
"Yes."

I could hardly believe my eyes. Who was this lady whose face exploded with love and aliveness? Was she the one I had asked for? Just two weeks ago I had begun to consider the possibility of a new relationship. At least I was willing to test the waters. I was clear I did not want anything remotely resembling the past. I was willing to have it all, or nothing.

I had realized, looking back at all my significant loving relationships, that each had gone through a birth/death cycle of its own. It seemed that relationships—as much as our bodies, cars, and clothes—had a built-in obsolescence factor that had to be overcome if one were to have a long-lasting, passionate bond. I knew that my thoughts in this area were a projection of the idea in my mind that everything has a beginning, middle and end, but I was now committed to seeing life in a different light—as a continuum of eternal moments, each of which is a new beginning.

But seeing and experiencing are two entirely different matters!

One thing I knew was that in the past my relationships had had an unconscious conception. I had stumbled into this one, bumped into the next, and collided into a third. I had never taken time to express my clarity of purpose in choosing a relationship in the first place. How could I expect anything but muddles when my conceptions were so foggy? And so I had vowed never to set my foot into a relationship until I was clear about the direction I was choosing to take. I would know what I wanted before I found myself in the middle of something I was all too familiar with for yet another time.

Thus had I sat down with pen and paper and initiated Step 1 of what later evolved into the *CREATE-A-MATE* system. On the top of the page I wrote the words, "MY IDEAL LOVING RELATIONSHIP," and I began to place my order, as it were. I was certain of what I *didn't*

artner, and I was willing to say no to that forever. But I had
asked myself what I *did* want, which, after all, is an important
part of the process.

You must be clear about what you want if only to recognize it
when it comes along. Normally, you attract what you are accustomed
to, maybe someone like your father, mother, brother, sister. To attract
someone truly extraordinary, you must first envision someone who
doesn't fit your pictures.

And so I had sat down with my pen and paper, getting my
values and priorities in order.

MY IDEAL LOVING RELATIONSHIPS

I'd like to be with a woman who is—
1. *happy*
2. *physically beautiful, preferably blonde*
3. *close to God*
4. *bright, intelligent, wise*
5. *passionate, alive, healthy, powerful*
6. *warm and friendly*
7. *self-sufficient (doesn't need a man!)*
8. *very intuitive and telepathic*
9. *likes sports*
10. *likes to travel*
11. *likes the arts*
12. *very loyal*
13. *peaceful*
14. *good relationship with her parents*
15. *good sense of humor.*

At the time I made my "shopping list," I was working with affirmations, or implants quite religiously (see my book *Open Heart Therapy*).
I was going through a period of growth where my mind needed an ex-
tensive overhaul. I had been brainwashed with so many lies, illusions
and myths about relationships that nothing short of a complete rewir-
ing of my mental circuits would do.

Just for fun I started writing two thoughts twenty times each per
day: *I now create my ideal loving relationship,* and *A wonderful surprise is just around
the corner.*

That had been two weeks ago. Now, looking into Mallie's eyes, I wondered if she was the answer to my prayers, a dream come true, or just another beautiful blonde. She seemed strangely familiar and yet unlike anyone I had ever known. It was interesting to me that she lived practically around the corner.

"Do you want to stay the night?"
"Yes."

The day I connected with Mallie, my life changed forever. Just looking at her I knew I would never be the same again. I had met my match. I was hooked.

What a terrifying prospect! No wonder I did everything possible to test the "pact" I felt.

You must understand, much as I thought I desired to create a mate, the possibility of succeeding at my mission had not really crossed my mind.

Moreover, Mallie and I were not kids when we met. Nor were we willing to grow old together. We had been married three times between us and had enjoyed our fair share of flings. We had no good reason to believe that the future of our relationships would be any better than the past.

Each of us had concluded separately that relationships were a necessary burden in life, pleasurable at times but not by nature, hardly a thing of joy and beauty. Relationships seemed to fall into two categories—either short-lived, passionate romances, or drawn-out, tedious struggles. Neither one seemed an attractive alternative. It was obvious to both of us: we didn't want a relationship like any we had ever seen, much less been in.

The only problem was what to do about this overwhelming desire to be together.

We had each been alone for several months, a long time for us. Neither one of us needed another relationship. We were happy in our separate lives, and whatever problems we did have seemed more easily resolvable alone than with someone. Relationships always complicate matters, we thought. In our early thirties, we both had finally gotten it together on our own, or, at least, were well on our way towards that goal.

"Do you want to stay the night?"
"Yes."

I couldn't explain my feelings to myself. I had "fallen" in love many times, but this felt altogether different, and far more frightening. I wasn't falling in any sense of the word. I didn't expect anyone to catch me, save me, rescue me or even help me.

I was fine alone. But looking into Mallie's bright eyes I was so much finer, as though her presence reminded me of how wonderful I was alone. The thought crossed my mind: *Maybe I'm rising in love!*

There was no logical way I could comprehend what I was feeling. I hardly knew the lady, yet my heart felt flooded with information about her. I could see not only her natural beauty, warmth, wisdom, honesty, wit, and many of the other qualities on my list, but also her love of children, animals, flowers, sunshine, and islands. I could see her whole life flash before my eyes.

It was like a very high drug experience. I could see who she was and she seemed like someone I had known forever, although I had never set eyes on her before. In fact, I had met her two months before but hadn't noticed who she was. Now I was completely enchanted! Past lives flashed before us. We could literally see the lifetimes of running away, chasing, leaving each other.

When Mallie and I connected, the special effects were stunning!

"Do you want to stay the night?" Mallie asked.
"Yes," I responded.

Where that *yes* came from I never have figured out. There was no part of my conscious mind that wanted to say yes to a woman at that moment. Nor was it lust or any other common denominator. Moreover, I knew Mallie had two daughters, and I assumed she was married. And I was not in the habit of making it with unhappy wives, especially when I was practicing celibacy.

This *yes* seemed to explode from the core of my being, as the question had popped out of Mallie's mouth before she knew what she was saying. An unknown me was saying *yes* to an unknown her.

It is this deep sense of mystery that always draws us closer and perhaps helps to explain the overwhelming desire to be together.

What to do! What to do! On the one hand, there was a driving desire to be together. On the other hand, the voice of experience said that relationships don't work, they're hopeless, the good times never last, what's the point?

Why a relationship? I thought. Why box the love in a limited container?

You can't possess love anyway. That seemed to be the trouble for most people. They found this wonderful, eternal, immeasurable thing called love, and almost immediately they would try to contain it, possess it, hold on to it—as though love were something you can deposit in a savings account and then withdraw when you need it.

Love, it seemed to me, was fluid like a river. You could never put your foot in the same spot twice. All there was was the experience. You can't have love like you have a car, a house or a TV. Love is ultimately formless.

As I looked at Mallie, lifetimes of running gripping my legs, the same question came up for both of us: Why a relationship? Why not just love?

Still, there was this overwhelming desire to be together.

My legs were wobbly. My hands were sweaty. This *yes* was reverberating through every cell of my body. It felt more like I was breaking up with someone I had been with for years; hardly love at first sight! Was there a difference finally between the first and last moments of a relationship? Was the fear of loss there from the starting gate? And if loss was inevitable, why start in the first place?

Yet the love was immeasurable. There was no beginning or end to it. It felt boundless, infinite. It has always been, and could no more die than the universe itself could putter out. The love was so gargantuan that there was, finally, no fear of loss, just of overwhelm!

Even though I had said *yes,* every muscle in my body wanted to bolt out the door. I couldn't, however. I was in the middle of teaching a seminar. In Mallie's living room! The break was almost over. I was clearly trapped!

The topic of the seminar was Rebirthing: A Simple Breathing Process. I don't think I breathed the rest of the evening. I remember talking very quickly, racing through my notes to complete the evening. God, was I thirsty!

It was February 22, 1977, the birthday of my relationship with Mallie.

When the seminar was over and everyone had cleared out, I found I was still glued to the rocker where I had sat all evening. Mallie sat down on the couch and lit a cigarette. I think I was drawn to her lack of purity. A cigarette can symbolize so many things to so many people. At that time it signified a flaw, a sign of humanity, as well as a grounded Mother Earthiness.

She smiled and I instantly knew we could be great friends forever. If it weren't for this overwhelming desire to be with her. I moved to sit with her on the couch.

"I don't usually ask men to stay the night," said Mallie.

"I don't usually say yes," I responded.

"I don't even know what happened," she added.

"Neither do I."

"I don't want a relationship."

"Neither do I."

"I can't think of one good reason to have a relationship."

"Neither can I."

And so it went. For five days we continued this conversation about not having a relationship. Each of us would share a negative thought about relationships, and the other would instantly agree, then add another thought to the pot.

"Women are too dependent," I said.

"Right," agreed Mallie. "And men are too withholding."

"Absolutely," I agreed. "And women are covert."

"I know," Mallie nodded. "And men are controlling."

"True," I confirmed. "And women are so smothering."

"For sure," Mallie agreed again. "And men run off."

It was quite a process—a process I'd recommend to any new couple. What we were doing was sharing all our negative thoughts about being together. We put all our cards on the table. It was a riot. I never laughed, cried, or shook so much in my life. Every time I uttered a new thought, I could feel my love for Mallie swell up more forcefully. Expressing the fear seemed to make room for the love.

The more we acknowledged our fear of relationships, the more we experienced the safety in choosing to be together. In the middle of it all, I asked God what the purpose of relationships was—Why be with anyone?

I remembered a phrase my father used whenever I asked him why he had business partners. "Two heads are better than one!" he'd say. *TWO HEARTS ARE BETTER THAN ONE,* I thought. I wanted to be with Mallie because I intuitively knew my life would be easier, happier, and generally better than alone, good as that had become.

When two self-sufficient, satisfied individuals surrender to being mutually interdependent, the seed of a good relationship takes root. This seems to be the key to all healthy relationships, be they romantic, business, or plain old-fashioned friendships. All your relationships should make your life easier, and what makes your life easier is good for your health.

Ultimately, people are good for each other!

Love can be a terrifying prospect. On the one hand, we seem to want it more than anything. On the other hand, it brings up anything unlike itself, and often we want to run away from "the dark side of love." Falling in love is not the answer because "falling" for someone is usually the expression of a hopeless longing to have someone take care of you forever, which is not the stuff great relationships are made of.

"Rising in love" is a much better solution. When two people who love themselves choose to be together, there is twice as much love for each of them. Most relationships begin unconsciously, and when the conception of anything is off, how can the fruition be anything but flawed? So the first step is to get clear on what you want so you recognize it when it comes along. (Your mind is so accustomed to what it doesn't want that it has to be trained to see what it really desires but is unaccustomed to receiving.) The second step is, once you do attract that perfect partner, to sit down and tell each other all your fears. Get through the terror fast! Allow the love to replace the fear and build the habit of telling the truth fast from day one of your relationship.

THE END
OF THE RUNWAY

"Why don't you go jump out the window?"
"I would, but I can't fly!"

When I was a kid, I had a recurring dream. Or was it a dream?

I'd be lying on my bed, staring at the shadows on the ceiling—shadows caused by the friendly flickering of streetlights and passing cars below.

We lived on the fourth floor of a typical apartment building in a typical section of Brooklyn. I'd stare at those ghostly shadows, and my child-mind would play games with their changing forms. One moment I'd see a big black banana; the next it'd be a big black cat, or a tiger, or an elephant. Or those big black flowers—''night flowers,'' I'd call them—that only showed their blossoms after the sun set and the city went to sleep, disappearing in the morning as mysteriously as they had appeared the previous evening. Or the Big Bad Man, who wore a trench coat and would slide down off the ceiling, down the wall, standing hugely over my bed for the sole purpose, I was certain, of scaring the living daylights out of me, my eyes squeezed tightly shut.

And so I serenaded myself to sleep among the shadows each night.

I was not a happy kid. One of the sources of my endless, or so I thought, misery, was my father's refusal to move out of the city. I remember lying among the shadows, praying that I would wake up in the country the next morning, that my night flowers would become day flowers, and that my kingdom of imaginary creatures would become a real farm with real animals and real crops to harvest.

Actually, I would have settled for a house on Long Island. Anything to leave the city!

Anyway, there was this recurring dream, or something. I'd be lying on my bed, eyes closed to protect me from the Big Bad Man, when suddenly my breath would sail out of my body and—without any further ado—I'd be on the ceiling, like one of those shadows, staring down at my body.

I was so light, it was all I could do to keep my balance. It was like falling upwards. If the ceiling had not been there, I was certain I would have "fallen" all the way to the moon.

At first these "dreams" were terrifying, but also somehow exciting, thrilling. After a while, when I learned how to control my "flying," it became fun. I learned how to use my breath to regulate my altitude and my arms and legs to keep my balance. I could now maneuver myself across the ceiling quite adeptly. I was a little Superboy learning how to use my powers.

I was ready to jump out the window!

With some trepidation I navigated myself to the window one night, where I hung out for a minute or two, deciding on a flight plan, and then I really took off. At first I just buzzed around near the window, like I had seen the pigeons do, but as I gained more courage and certainty, I'd explore the whole street, neighborhood, Brooklyn and, eventually, all of New York City. This took me several nights to accomplish.

I can still remember the thrill, the breeze slapping against my face, the stars and the moon and the Empire State Building, the trees (they grow in Brooklyn, mostly in Prospect Park) and the birds and the Statue of Liberty.

God, how I loved to fly!

"Why don't you go jump out the window?"
"I would, but I can't fly!"

I've been a leaver all my life. Maybe because my dad never would move to the Island. (He promised my mom that after they retired they would have enough money to travel in style and spend the rest of their days in the world's finest hotels—a promise he never did keep.) Maybe there was a part of me that wanted to fulfill my dad's unfinished dreams. Or maybe it was just to protect myself from my greatest fear—of women abandoning me—that I would choose to leave first. Whatever it was, leaving was all I knew and all I had ever known.

When the going got rough, I would fly off. To work, to other women, to travel, to move, or, perhaps even more profoundly, within myself, to secret shelves of my being where no one could find me. "Fifty Ways to Leave Your Lover" was not only my favorite song, it seemed to be based on my emotional itinerary, if not my actual history.

Born, bred and educated in New York City, I left when I was 23 to live in Cleveland, New Haven, Stockholm, London, San Francisco, Bucks County, Trenton and Santa Fe, New Mexico. For me, leaving was like chasing those shadows on my ceiling, then flying up to join them, then taking off out the window.

I just couldn't stay put. It seemed like my feet had a fate of their own, and that I was doomed to go along for the ride. One summer I drove cross-country three times. I got married in the middle and never could get out. The day my father died I was driving through a hurricane in southern Mexico. I also remember the day my house in Bucks County burned down, turning a piece of my marriage into ashes. I remember leaving my wife in Santa Fe to return to New York and setting it up so the marriage wouldn't survive the journey. I saw what it means to be a heel, to leave those you love in your footsteps.

I had vowed never to live in New York City again. To me it represented the pain of the childhood I was trying to escape. The more I travelled, however, the more I discovered that while I could leave New York, that did not mean the city would leave me. It was when I lived in Europe that I came to experience my love for my motherland (and my mother) and how blest all Americans are, whether they know it or not. And it was when I came back to New York to make my peace with my past that I began to see new possibilities for my future.

I had flattered myself by calling myself a free spirit. Actually, I had a fierce leaving pattern—something I had to handle if I wanted my relationship with Mallie to be like no other. And to last.

Mallie had this amazing staying power. Not only had she stayed in an unhappy marriage for 13 years—to a man more in love with sailing than staying—staying was in her blood! Her family was hearty Vermont stock. They had stayed in the tiny town of East Arlington, Vermont, since pre-revolutionary days. To listen to her dad was to hear a veritable Homeric tale of people, places, and events of three centuries mixed together, like rope in his mind.

Mallie's family—the Mattisons—were like rocks. All they knew was how to stay put. Oh, occasionally one of them would roll off somewhere, but basically they were real settled in their ways. If you had a map of their mind, it would be like one of those New Yorker magazine maps with East Arlington in the middle, stretching clear up to Burlington, way down to New York, out west to Albany and far east to Boston. The rest of the world would probably appear in a small square like they show Hawaii or Alaska on most maps of the states.

The Mattisons had *roots!* Mallie's transplant to New York City was about as far as a girl could go. (Mallie had to leave the country as I had to leave the city.)

The Mandels, on the other hand, had *routes!* Immigrants, all of us, we were always looking for a better life, a new world, a promised land. As wandering Jews from Germany and czarist Russia, emigration was a way of life for us. My mom came over on a boat when she was six months old—in 1905 when Russia was starting to rumble at its core. Her dad had deserted the Czar's army six months earlier, to make a new life for his new wife and daughter, and set sail for America—the Columbus of my family.

No wonder my dad wanted to stay put. (He would fly off the handle or out the door to smoke a cigar.) But flying was in my blood as surely as staying was in Mallie's.

We had a lot to share, the two of us, lifetimes to catch up on, and family traditions that needed merging if we were to become one blood, one thread.

All this was somewhat complicated by the fact that one of the first agreements Mallie and I made was: *No family obligations!* By which we meant that neither of us would hold the other accountable for the other's family, be it in the form of weddings, funerals, or family get-togethers of any sort. In all our previous relationships, family expectations, entanglements, and obligations had caused us considerable grief.

If you stop to think about it, relationships with in-laws are perhaps the most unnatural and induced relationships we ever experience. You choose to be with one person—a difficult enough choice in the first place—and whammo, there you are, suddenly a member of a whole new family—lock, stock and barrel. Nothing short of birth itself exposes you to such intense observation, judgment, and scrutiny by a group of people you never consciously chose to be with. Which is not to say that some people don't find the acceptance they never found in their natural family with their in-laws.

Allowing our relationships with each other's families the breathing room to grow organically was not always easy. Sometimes it seemed to tear our guts apart. But, in the long run, it seems to have produced a genuine sense of chosen family among us all.

The merger of the ''roots'' with the ''routes'' was a lesson in patience and persistence!

"Why don't you go jump out the window?"
"I would, but I can't fly!"

You must understand, when I first met Mallie I had just reached that point of life where I had become my number one priority. No more sacrifice. No more martyrdom. Of course, since I was so out of balance on this whole issue, I unfortunately seemed often cold, callous, and cruel in saying no to others. But I believed in the process of reclaiming my personal power. I knew it was the only way to go. And I was determined to let nothing interfere!

UNTIL YOU ARE COMMITTED TO YOUR OWN WELL-BEING, THE POSSIBILITY OF COMMITMENT TO A RELATIONSHIP IS PREMATURE!

What *is* commitment anyway? It's not the same as agreement, where two people basically mistrust each other and therefore hold each other accountable for a given course of action. "You gave me your word!" is the voice of agreement.

"You gave me your heart!" is the voice of commitment. Commitment is a deep trust, a devotion discovered in the choice to be together. Commitment needs no agreements because it is based on desire, not obligation.

What I used to call freedom now seems like pure escapism to me. I used to believe I was free to the extent that I avoided structure in life. In the name of freedom, I withheld choosing, committing, or devoting myself fully to anything. I was rebelling from control, be it a steady job, a permanent home, or an everlasting relationship.

I was committed to non-commitment!

I would drift through life, flow with it, and take what life tossed my way. I didn't know that my flow was being governed by subconscious programming I was denying and suppressing. I didn't know that until you *choose* what you really want in life, you tend to drift in the same recurrent circles endlessly. My basic attitude was that if it works out, I'll choose it.

I was frozen in suspended animation. A free spirit? Hardly! I hovered above my options in life like a frightened bird, never diving fully into anything for fear I'd drown, suffocate, or be eternally trapped in a choice I'd later regret. I'd seen too many people stuck in the bitter results of past choices. I was not about to make the same mistakes. Not me. I was too smart.

In the course of time I came to see how stupid my smartness was. I saw how in not choosing I was selling out. I wasn't even choosing life, let alone participating in it. I saw my relationships fail one after another because I set them up that way. Because I never chose them. Because I had this "wait and see" attitude. Because I was watching my own life pass me by. Because, whether I knew it or not, I was choosing to be alone.

I had to admit how much I feared entrapment and what that was all about. How what I was calling freedom was fear in disguise. I came to be rebirthed—to re-experience the walls of my mother's uterus closing in on me the bigger I grew in the last trimester of pregnancy. It was as though all the memories were still there, lodged in the cells of my body, only a few breaths away . . . . I felt how this primal "no exit" terror was the driving force in my delivery, and how subconsciously I thought that leaving was the only way to go in life, that my survival depended on it, and that it was the source of my spiritual deliverance too! I realized that all my battles with women were but minor skir-mishes—symbols of The Great War with my mother, the war I had entered in my own mind at my own birth when I erroneously decided that to stay was to die and to leave was to live. I even got to see how my love for my mom—and all women—was so great, I would sooner leave than hurt them. I have since come to call this primal conflict *The Infant Guilt Syndrome*, which I believe to be the cause of much misery in later life (see my book *Open Heart Therapy*).

> *"Why don't you go jump out the window?"*
> *"I would, but I can't fly!"*

And so I came to the end of the runway. That point where it seemed I had only two options in life, to fly off, or to crash. And neither of these options was acceptable, because I had now met Mallie, and there was this overwhelming desire to be together.

I was committed to myself. That much I knew. In staying that first night with Mallie I already knew that I had planted a seed that could grow into something extraordinary. On the other hand, perhaps it would turn into a Venus flytrap.

When I thought of Mallie's family—her two daughters (Kim and Susie) and her parents and her four brothers and their wives and their children—it was a bit much for my mind to handle. So I tried to keep the whole clan out of my mind.

I remember the time Mallie's grandmother was dying in Vermont. I was leading a workshop in nearby Massachusetts. I refused to accompany Mallie to visit her family. I wanted *to want* to go with her, but I didn't. I couldn't. It felt too much like an obligation, a trap. I had to choose me, guilty though I felt.

I remember other times when Mallie and the girls drove up to Vermont and I'd sit home doing nothing. I had no good reason not to go. I thought I was defending a principle. I was also seeing the limits of my commitment to Mallie.

There were other times I'd go to Vermont and sit among the clan and wonder what planet I was on. I'd listen to her father ramble on in an eternal monologue about people I never heard of. I'd listen to her brothers talk fishing, hunting, or heavy duty machinery and I'd think, *What on God's earth has brought me here?* Many times I could not even understand the words behind their accents.

But there was a process at work here. Every time I chose to be with Mallie's family, I felt freer to be *me* with them. Since I knew I didn't have to be with them, I began to *want* to be with them. And the more I chose Mallie, the more I chose her whole life—past, present, and future. And the more I chose her family, the less they seemed like strangers and the more they seemed like . . . well, family.

It became obvious: in choosing I was free and in not choosing I was stuck, and every moment of my life was a crossroads. There is no preconceived map of life to follow. There is no "path"! God has not designed your flight plan. You are free! A friend once told me, "There is no escape from freedom!" You carve your path as you go by choosing and learning. You veer this way and that, seeing the consequences of your choices and changes. Mathematically, the shortest distance between two points is said to be a straight line, but human destiny is not so simply measured. Sometimes a human being takes the long route because in the end it proves shorter!

"Why don't you go jump out the window?"
"I would, but I can't fly!"

And then there were children! There had been times in my life when I had felt a deep drive to have my own children. There were other times when it seemed the last thing in the world I wanted. I was enough of a child for me to handle. Usually I thought I would have children when I was ready. But never in my wildest dreams did I anticipate being ready for two powerful young ladies, aged eight and ten, and not of my own seed. Kim was always easy for me. She was older when her parents separated. Much as it tore her up, on some level she understood it had to be, it was best for both of them. When I came into the picture, Kim saw me as someone who could make her mother happy, and she knew that the happier Mallie was, the better it would be for her.

Kim and I recognized each other instantly. There was a whole lot of love very soon. My main problem was handling all the love she gave me—what had I done to deserve it? I wasn't even her real dad.

We had our fights, Kim and I. But they were fortunately infrequent, and, because we hated hating each other even for a moment, we'd always end up crying in each other's arms.

God, how I love Kim. She is incredibly beautiful, physically and spiritually. She is alive, vibrant, excited, eager, brilliant, and extremely gifted. She is in many ways "the good girl" as Suzie is the rebel. But labels are false for any individuals. And Kim and Suzie are individuals if they are anything!

I love Kim's own loving relationship. She and Robert have been together for two years as I write, and it is amazing to me how sweet and good they are together. I never knew people their age could be so advanced. I think it scares them to be so beautiful together so soon in life. They never take their future for granted, but they deal with their fears and anxieties so honestly. And there is this sense of always-ness about them. What most astounds and delights me is the quality of the friendship behind their romance. Kim is a temperamental fire. Robert is a wise old log. Together they create warmth. Sometimes sparks fly.

Every morning of the first month I lived with Mallie, Suzie (our eight-year-old) would ask me the same question, "Why don't you go jump out the window?" And I would give her the same answer, "I would, but I can't fly!"

With Suzie, sparks flew all the time. Every day was July 4th. Fireworks. Independence Day! She was a born rebel and challenged my male ego beyond its frail fringes. In tempting me to jump out the window she was saying: *If you're going to leave sooner or later, beat it!* She was angry at her father for leaving, and she had no qualms at all about taking it out on me. She was eight years old and easily the greatest challenge of my life. She began to represent every woman who had ever rejected me, all rolled into one. It was years before she told me she loved me, let alone hugged or kissed me.

And yet it was Suzie who stole my heart. There was something between us that made each of us know we had met our match. In relating to her I could feel what my Dad must have felt about me as a child, when I was so angry and belligerent, but alive and excited. Suzie was a female reflection of what I was like at her age. And at times I found the reflection unacceptable.

If the fights with Kim were lover's quarrels, the war with Suzie was primal jungle warfare—the kind of combat God's beasts engage in before becoming one family.

Kim taught me how to receive love, Suzie how to give it. I could never be sure I'd get anything in exchange for what I gave Suzie. I just knew it was the right thing for me to do. She was like a cornered, wounded animal. I had to learn the art of loving from a distance. But I always knew that in loving her unconditionally, I would somehow be healed deeply in my soul.

There was always a strong psychic connection with Suzie. We'd read each other's minds, finish each other's sentences, and think of the same jokes at the same time. Sometimes she'd unconsciously act out my worst fears. I'd be worrying about money, and she'd ask for a raise in her allowance or money for new clothes or jewelry. She always taught me that I could afford to be generous and that the more I provided for my family, the more prosperous I would become. At the same time, she gave me a very valuable lesson in saying no to those I love.

Suzie is one of God's undiscovered masterpieces. She is at once 16 and 42 and 9 and 2. Her age cannot be measured in years. Nor can her wisdom. And her heart can be with you or without you in the blink of an eye. The kid is lightning.

One thing that always amazed me about Mallie was how she stepped aside to let me get close to her children. She let it happen. She rarely got in the middle. She was secure in her relationship to them and insisted that I make my own bond with them and they with me. She inspired us to work out our differences in the context of one family, and she made it quite clear to the kids that I was here to stay. This created a sense of inevitability about our all surrendering to each other. When the going got real rough, we'd have a family powwow, air our grievances and strengthen our connection. Over time, the kids came to see that I was on their side as much as their mother.

Now I realize that children can come to parents in many ways, and that all of God's ways are equally natural. These are my children and always will be—by choice if not by blood. By heart for sure. If I am a step-parent—a phrase I abhor—it is only because I chose to step towards children reaching out for love. It was the most gigantic step of my life.

Because I had this fierce leaving pattern, I had always looked for the easy way out. Now I came to see that the easy way out was often to stay. It was only when I fully chose to stay that my life really took off.

Freedom is not always what it appears to be! Although we value freedom next to life itself, how often do we exercise our freedom? Often, in the name of being "a free spirit," we paralyze ourselves in not choosing. We withhold ourselves from the many options open to us, thinking if we choose one thing fully—be it a career, a home, a relationship—it eliminates our other options. Actually, we are terrified of entrapment and abandonment, and commitment seems to activate these memories from birth faster than anything. We project our subconscious impressions of "no exit terror" onto our relationships, then think we have to leave in order to continue to live and grow. This primal panic we bring to love makes our relationships crazy from the start. The solution is to be committed to your own well-being first, then to your partner's. The more you choose to be yourself, your full and holy self, in all your relationships, the more you discover your natural commitment to those you love. "You gave me your word!" is the voice of agreement. "You gave me your heart!" is the voice of commitment. You discover your commitment, and then your devotion, by choosing to stay day by day. And as you choose to let go of your reactive personality in favor of your intuitive self, you come to see that the only thing that has ever stood in your way is what you have suppressed from your past. When you make peace with your past, your future takes off.

BROKEN GLASSES!

"What is she doing?"
"She's throwing glasses against the wall."

Mallie was working as Assistant Director for Manhattanville Community Center. She had a nine-to-five job. I was just beginning my career in the self-improvement business. My hours were my own.

Every morning Mallie would get up, make the kids breakfast, send them off to school, then go to work. I would be left alone in this strange apartment where Mallie and her husband had lived for 13 years.

I was still married to Kathy. Mallie was still married to Steve.

I remember my first morning alone in that place. As Mallie was leaving, she reminded me to help myself to the refrigerator. We hugged for a long time. (We had not yet made love.) Then she left. I never felt so uncomfortable in my life. For a while I sneaked and skulked about the apartment like an intruder, a burglar, someone who didn't belong. It was one of those typical upper West Side apartments—in a pre-war building with a post-war view of 106th St. I examined every nook and cranny, half expecting to find some long-buried family secret, half waiting for someone to discover my presence and ask me what right I had to be there.

"Well, er, you see, sir, I really am in the right place. . . . I was invited, yes, I am a guest. . . . I might, er, even stay."

Finally, I made my way to the refrigerator. The kitchen was miniscule and the refrigerator was in the dining room, which was not much larger. I opened the refrigerator door, looked at the family store, took out a bottle of fruit juice and walked back to the kitchen to pour myself a glass.

"What is she doing?"
"She's throwing glasses against the wall."

I no sooner lifted a glass than it slid through my hand and shattered into a hundred little pieces. I jumped back, horrified by my mess, my clumsiness. I waited, held my breath, making sure no one would discover me. I felt eyes upon me.

Who was this ghost I thought was watching me? What did I owe the Spirits of the Past?

I quickly swept up the pieces of glass and deposited them in the trash. Then I reached for another glass and it too was a shattering experience.

I dropped three glasses in all. I began to think I was a jinx to Mallie and the children, that I would somehow bring them bad luck (or they me), and should "get on the bus, Gus," better leave town.

These glasses were amazing! They seemed to have a will of their own—thoughts and power to propel them. They literally jumped out of my hand, one after the other, kamikaze pilots crashing to smithereens.

Later I realized who the ghosts were and how to do exorcisms, for people must be exorcised of their pasts if their spirits are to be united. And places must be purged of their histories if the space is to be fresh for new love. Objects also have power—the power of the people who handled them. In moving to Mallie's home, I not only had to face the merger of two diametrically opposed family traditions, but there were physical memories we were bringing together, memories contained in sentimental objects, relics of past relationships, remnants of lost love and reminders of what once was or might have been.

There was no place for nostalgia in the relationship Mallie and I were planning. How could we long for the past when the present was so magical? How could we cling to lost dreams when the current reality was the ultimate dream come true.

We were so much in love, so much and so fast a part of each other, that our separate histories, our separate routes made little sense except that they had led us to this magnificent moment in time. We wanted to let go of the past. We knew we had to. And we knew we had never done it before.

The process was one of cutting hundreds of little—and big—energy cords that had gone out from us to other people, places, and things in our lives. We had to reclaim all that lost hope, summon back the dreams, in order to bond and blend with each other with all our heart.

Two hearts are better than one. But the two hearts must be free of all past contracts.

Sweeping up the last three glasses, I began to think of cleaning up my past—especially with my mom and ex-wife.

I thought of the glasses and how many times Mallie and Steve must have drunk from them, and suddenly I didn't want them in "my" house any more. I let myself feel possessive of the physical space I was choosing to call home. I let my territoriality take over, like an animal staking its ground. I wanted to get rid of every glass from Mallie's past, and my own. I would smash them all! I wanted to make it all brand new.

"What is she doing?"
"She's throwing glasses against the wall."

I remembered an old Mexican friend of mine who, whenever he got stuck in life, would heave beer bottles against brick walls, shattering the glass until his anger was spent.

There were many forms of broken glass I had to sweep up. Most immediate was completing it with my soon-to-be-ex-wife, Kathy. Our marriage had ended with many bad feelings, and I somehow had to take the bull by the horns and wrestle that beast to sleep. Looking back at what had happened, I felt deep remorse for my clandestine behavior towards the end.

I remember writing Kathy a long letter, a completion letter as we call it in the trade. At the time I thought it was a brilliant epistle. Looking back, it was pure enlightened horsebleep. I certainly took the enlightened approach in this letter. I "owned" the mess I created; I took complete responsibility for my part; I forgave Kathy her contribution; I could see the utter perfection of it all; it was God's will, fate, destiny, karma—you name it, I passed the buck to it.

My intention was honest enough. But my technique was just a new version of my old need to be self-righteous, arrogant, and pompous. Even in admitting I had been wrong, I had somehow written a letter defending my right-ness. Hell, now I even had God on my side.

The truth was that I was incredibly guilty for sabotaging my marriage. And until I confronted my guilt directly I was in no position to experience my innocence.

Nonetheless, I mailed my masterpiece to San Francisco where, if any little piece of my heart remained, I hoped it would be returned to me A.S.A.P.

I waited and I waited, and I waited, but no reply ever came. I began to see how invested I was in a response. I realized that my motive in writing the letter had been all wrong, that I had wanted Kathy's approval and forgiveness when I could not give it to myself.

REDEMPTION CANNOT COME FROM SOMEONE ELSE! FORGIVENESS, LIKE CHARITY, BEGINS AT HOME!

I first had to forgive myself for ruining my marriage. Kathy's forgiveness was secondary and ultimately irrelevant. Looking at the broken glass on Mallie's kitchen floor, I remembered the happy times with Kathy, when we lived peacefully in Bucks County, when I was writing and she was dancing; the times in Santa Fe when we were in love with the land and the sky; the times we camped in the Redwoods spending whole days in silent harmony. In remembering the good days and letting go of the bad ones, I somehow felt more resolved about everything.

There was, however, one last incompletion. I owed Kathy some money her mother had loaned us during the hard times that tended to characterize our time together. The amount was not huge. I certainly could now afford to pay her back. But I kept procrastinating the final payment. It was as though I held on to this last debt as a sentimental token of our love. To let it go felt like letting go of Kathy forever. Finally, I did it! I was in San Francisco on a business trip. I met Kathy and we walked to the Gibraltar Bank on 24th Street in Noe Valley, where I kept my West Coast account. I made the necessary withdrawal and gave her the cash. It was very emotional. It freed me. It was like saying good-bye to my guilt, to everything I ever thought I owed that marriage, to every thought I ever had of saving it. It was like taking my heart back from San Francisco.

People hold on to the past in many subtle, covert, and unconscious ways. I see couples split up and leave all kinds of loose ends in each other's possession. Entirely innocent, they don't realize the dire consequences of saving old pictures, old love letters, old clothing, or even wearing a ring given as a pledge of a permanent bond. Not to mention the emotional ties they refuse to shed—whether it's incomplete grief for a dead parent or held resentment towards an ex-mate.

Remember, your word is the law in the physical universe. If you gave your word to someone, if you promised you would always be together, that is a contract you've made and must annul—mentally, spiritually, and emotionally—if you are to be free for someone new. Old pacts with old lovers hold you back, no matter how old and insignificant they seem to your conscious mind.

"What is she doing?"
"She's throwing glasses against the wall."

My mother was another glass that needed throwing.

I have always loved my mother, and she me. She is an incredible woman. The oldest of four children, she dropped out of high school and went to work when she was thirteen. She worked for the Jewish Family Service for over fifty years. She retired three times and unretired twice. (Finally, they hired three people to do the one job.) She raised two powerful children and was a tower of strength and support for my father. In addition to her power and endurance, my mom is full of love, passion, wisdom, common sense and humor. She is one of a kind.

Unfortunately, I hardly noticed many of my mother's virtues while I was growing up. I was too busy rebelling from what, to me, looked like her smotherly vices. I felt too sheltered, protected, and guarded by her love. I wanted to break out, see the world, take risks, learn from my own dumb mistakes. Like any parent, she wanted to save me the pain, show me the shortcuts, stop me when she saw me headed blindly and bullishly towards a brick wall. In my mind she was my greatest obstacle to freedom. In her mind she didn't want me to hurt myself.

And so that primal tug of war became an adolescent's fight for his independence.

I remember the first time I was rebirthed. I was lying down, breathing away, my body vibrating with wave after wave of energy, remembering the cold, windy day I was born, how my dad forgot my mom's coat when it was time to take us home. Suddenly, the phone rang; the rebirther answered it and, God knows why, handed it to me.

"It's your mother."

I grabbed the phone.

"Hi, Mom."

"Hello, Bob, are you alright?"

"Yes, I'm alright."

"Oh, I just thought I'd call . . . You sound funny. What are you doing?"

"I'm getting rebirthed."

"Rebirthed? What's the matter, the first time wasn't good enough?"

My mother always seemed to disapprove of my far-out ways. She wanted me to be a doctor or a lawyer or a teacher or a social worker, something she could at least explain to her friends. It hurt me not to be able to give her this. I felt guilty and defensive. (Over the years, as my mother has participated in more and more of my workshops, her disapproval has turned to pride. We now both acknowledge that family service is an interest we share in common.)

Once I had the brilliant idea of firing my mother. I was 33 years old, a grown man; she had done her job of parenting to the best of her abilities; she deserved to be relieved of her duties. I thought I'd transform the parent-child relationship into a friendship. I called her up.

"Mom?"

"Yes?"

"You're fired."

"What?"

"You're fired as a mother. Your job's done. I'm all grown up."

"Are you alright?"

"Yes, I'm alright. I just want to be friends now. Okay?"

"Okay. We'll just be friends."

"Great."

"Did you call your sister?"

In a sense, a parent is forever. The immortality of the parent-child relationship is unquestionable, both biologically and emotionally. But there comes a time when parents and children must acknowledge their equality as human beings, grappling with similar life problems, if in dissimilar ways. This ability to make friends with your parents is often a key step in freeing you to bond with a mate. So often I counsel people—of all ages—who still seem to be waiting for their parents to give them some mysterious freedom they think is owed to them. Nonsense. Set your parents free. Give them the unconditional love you always wanted. Stop trying to change them. Your parents are perfect just the way they are!

"What is she doing?
"She's throwing glasses against the wall."

The big bang with my mom came one day in the summer of 1979. I had decided to tell her the truth. To suppress my feelings was no longer bearable. It was taking its toll on me and Mallie. Whatever you don't express to your parents you tend to dump on your mate, and it was time to change the game again.

I went to see my mother with the clear intention to release my anger. I knew it wouldn't take long to find an excuse to blast her, poor woman, and I was right. I had not been in her apartment for five minutes when I found a good enough reason to explode.

I remember the scene as clear as yesterday. We were standing three or four feet apart—I was careful not to invade her immediate energetic space (eighteen inches, psychologists say). I placed myself at a slight angle to her because I didn't want to vent my rage directly on her. I really was interested in release, not blame. I took complete responsibility as I shouted:

"I am angry . . . it's not your fault, it's in my body, it's my anger, but I hated you when you did . . . I can't stand it when you say . . . It hurts me when you do . . . I have never forgiven you for the time you . . ."

On and on it went, for ten or fifteen minutes. I never looked her in the eye. I cried as I screamed. It was intense.

When I felt complete, I took a few deep breaths and looked up. I had never seen my mother's eyes, tearful though they were, so radiant, so alive with love. "Bob," she said to me, "I'm so happy you let it all out. I always knew you had it locked up inside."

Mothers! They are the best therapists. They all have a direct pipeline to their children's hidden hearts. What's the point in trying to separate from them? Their telepathic connection is infallible.

I used to think my mother was neurotic and depressed. And, sure enough, whenever we were together, she would grow somber and morose.

One day I was visiting her when the phone rang and I picked up the receiver. It was an old friend of my mom's, someone I had grown up loving and respecting. After some preliminary chit-chat, she began to tell me how wonderful my mother was, how she was a delight to go out with, how funny she was, how she was always the life of the party.

Who was she talking about?

I began to see my mother was only depressed in the presence of my low thoughts about her. People tend to be chameleons, taking on the behavior most familiar to the people they're with. Not only do children often act out the subconscious minds of their parents; parents tend to fulfill their children's expectations of them as well!

I began to envision my mother in a different light. I imagined her joyful and playful, as I had known her to be in her youth. I planted the following thought in the garden of my subconscious mind, "My mother is a joy to be with!"

In a few weeks my relationship with my mom took another wonderful turn. We were laughing and playing, meeting for lunch, a drink, dinner. Just recently, we took her to our new home in Mykonos. She blew our minds with her boundless energy and excitement. At eighty! How young at heart she is!

My dad was a more difficult glass to shatter. He had died before I had the opportunity to heal it with him. My feelings towards him were very mixed up. On the one hand, I appreciated his non-intervention policy towards children. I knew he loved me. I knew he wanted me to live my own life, be free, discover for myself. (I'm sure he would have also loved it had I grown up to play centerfield for the Brooklyn Dodgers.) I knew he had been beaten by his father and that the last thing he wanted was to hurt me, which he never did—physically. At the same time, I had enormous resentment for the remoteness his fear of hurting me caused. I was mad because he had backed off so much he often seemed like an absentee dad.

I wrote him a long letter, pouring my heart out on paper. I cried, I screamed, I pounded the table, I tore up pages, I wrote and I re-wrote and I edited until I had a letter that I would not have minded receiving. (I had learned my lesson from my letter to Kathy.)

Mind you, I did all this knowing I never would receive a response. My dad was dead, floating up there in the ethers. And dead men don't write back. I wrote this letter for *me*, because I knew in forgiving him I would free myself to be the man I wanted to be. If the sins of the father are visited upon the son, it is for the son to forgive and thereby break the family curse.

I did it. I put the letter in an envelope and mailed it to:

Isidore Mandel
Heaven!

I omitted the return address!

What a difference it made! Almost immediately, I began to feel my father's presence return to my life. Mallie, who had never seen him and whom I knew he would have adored, began to see his spirit everywhere we went. She loved him. He became our guardian angel, in a sense. Also, my mom stopped complaining about him, which had been one of her favorite addictions.

I had never had many strong male friendships. All the men I loved tended to be remote like my dad. Or maybe I was the remote one.

As soon as I forgave my father, all kinds of wonderful men came into my life, and I was able to form deep, lasting bonds with brothers I had always craved. (I used to beg my parents to make a baby brother.)

My parents had always told me: Never marry a woman who didn't have good relationships with her parents. Twice I had rebelled from this idea, and twice I had ended up divorced. With Mallie, I hit the jackpot. She loved her mom and dad, and they her, in a way that always inspired me. And her parents' love for each other was as sweet as Kim's and Robert's. Of course, Mallie had things to clean up, too, and she went through her own process as I was going through mine. But all in all I felt honored to step into such sweetness. There's something to be said for good old Vermont maple syrup.

In cleaning it up with my parents, I was able to bring a fresh slate into my relationship with Mallie. The past was erased. At least, the bitterness was. We could therefore begin anew. This is what we mean when we tell people: Completion is a great place to start.

"What is she doing?" Susie asked me as we huddled in the middle of the living room floor.

"She's throwing glasses against the wall," I replied.

Mallie had locked herself in the bedroom and was smashing glass to vent her rage. She was always good at getting her anger out in safe ways. Sometimes she'd walk the dog. Sometimes she'd go jogging. She had this unique knack for handling emotions energetically. This particular time she chose to throw glasses.

As Susie and I listened to the glasses shatter, one by one, it seemed like all our emotions were shattering with the glass. Our bodies shook as we hugged each other. "Wait here," I finally told Susie, and I tiptoed to the bedroom where I knocked on the door. There was a moment of silence. Mallie opened the door slightly.

"Are you alright?" I asked.

"Of course I'm alright; I've never been better."

With that, she slammed the door and returned to her previous activity. When I returned to the living room, Susie asked me, "Is she alright?"

"Yes, she's alright."

No wonder Jews stomp on glasses when they get married. Or Greeks break dishes in the middle of the night. Or my Mexican friend threw beer bottles against brick walls.

However you do it, you have to crack the past to open the future.

A relationship is like a glass. Sometimes it's full; sometimes it's empty. More often, it is half full or half empty. You can see the fullness or the emptiness. The choice is yours. One thing for certain, however, is whichever way you choose to see it, so it will be. Whatever you focus on will expand.

Also, the more you fill up your glass, the more the crud rises to the surface. Which is why things sometimes get worse before they get better.

But, ultimately, you cannot contain love. Love is the water, flowing and free. Glass is the container, solid if transparent, something to hold on to.

Sometimes you have to shatter the glass and get yourself wet!

To forgive and let go of past pain is ultimately a self-serving choice. To hold on to old resentment and grievances is unhealthy—physically, mentally and spiritually. And that's what pain is—the effort involved in holding on to old, negative beliefs. People are terrified of forgiving because they think it will set them up to be hurt again. Your anger begins to feel like your personal power (instead of the helplessness it really is), and you use it to protect yourself from a world you have come to mistrust. The key to forgiving is (1) to own your blame and handle the energy physically, by breathing, jogging, throwing glasses, etc.; (2) to forgive yourself for creating the unpleasant situation; (3) to give up the desire to get even; and (4) to know you can forgive the other without setting up the same circumstances again. For example, if you have an employee who steals from your cash register, you might want to look at your own thoughts of mistrust and scarcity that he was acting out. You might also forgive your employee for his part in creating the theft. And you might want to fire the employee because you have legitimate reasons not to keep him at the cash register. To forgive is not to render yourself a blind fool. It is simply to release the incident so you can feel comfortable in that person's presence.

It is eminently practical to forgive your parents completely. They did the best they could. And the more you look at their relationships with their parents, the more you come to understand the choices they made. Also, the more you come to be in love with yourself, not to mention your perfect partner, the more you must inevitably come to the conclusion that, all in all, your parents did their job successfully.

24 HOURS
A DAY

"When are you going to quit?"
"Soon."

When I met Mallie, my life was moving very fast. To the un-trained eye, however, the movement hardly showed. Living with Mallie, my growth was accelerated, but I slowed down even more.

Such is life in the fast lane of enlightenment. Slowly is holy!

In fact, I hardly left the apartment for six months. For three months I rarely ventured from the bedroom. Remembering those days is like remembering an old, friendly dream. I can see myself lying in bed, or in the tub, breathing and tingling and sweating and sobbing—rebirthing, as we call it—using the breath to pump up the past and let go of the pain.

There was so much old hurt I was working on I didn't have much time for much else—like three meals a day, eight hours of sleep, a job, a car, money, manners. I was into this thing called "process," and weird as it seemed to outsiders it had a grip on me and I had to go through it.

And there were days I was high as a kite. Whether it was all that oxygen I was breathing or the energy it produced, or the emotional peaks, or the memories and realizations I was having—there were times I'd be flying on the right stuff.

Sometimes Mallie would hold me for hours, grounding my ecstasy in physical safety. We'd breathe together, our hearts opening, beating as one, laughing, crying, pulsating, bonding on a cellular level.

I remember once my mother called.

"You're breathing again."

"Yes, Mom."

"Why?"

"It feels good."

"Maybe I should breathe sometimes."

"It wouldn't hurt."

"Tell me, Bob, is it a cult?"

"No, Mother, it's not a cult."

"Is it a religion?"

"No, Mother, it's not a religion."

"What does it teach you?"

"It teaches that we are all divine beings."

"Divine beings? Hmmm. My son, the divine nut!"

Somehow this phrase stuck with me. I really thought of myself as a divine nut coming out of my shell. Later, when my mother told me I was delivered by Father Divine nurses (at a Jewish hospital), the primal joke of my life became clear.

I guess life is fair in the long run. One thing I know, however, is that there's never any gain without something being lost in the process, and what's lost is usually something we don't really want but are afraid to let go.

For me to surrender to this new life, this new energy, this new world coming through was to give up the world of respect for the "nut house" (which my mother assured me I was headed for). Not only did I lose a lot of friends who couldn't follow my changes, I lost a whole context for living that was as much a part of me as bagels and egg rolls and Prospect Park and Ebbets Field. I had been born and bred and educated for a physical universe, not a metaphysical one. I had attended Columbia and Yale, not to enter the realm of the unknown, but to succeed with known knowledge among knowledgeable people in a traditional world. I was to be a professional person—a doctor, a teacher, even a writer. But a new age seminar leader, an enlightened consultant, an intuitive counselor, a rebirther? Come on!

Little did they know!

The more I breathed, the more I discovered. The more I discovered, the more I wanted to share this process with others. I wanted to work in this field. It was a field of the future, a field of vision. For the first time in my life, I felt like I might have a calling, like maybe there was a God and maybe he had some purpose, after all, in breathing life into me. Maybe I wasn't a complete waste. I once saw a poster that said, *GOD DON'T MAKE JUNK!*

As I was realizing my potential value to others, I was looking worse than ever. Unshaved, undressed, and unkempt, I shuffled around the apartment, unfit to be seen, unprepared for daylight. You could say my internal growth had not yet expressed itself in my external presentation. You could also say I was a slob or a pig. A friend told me not to worry, I was just recovering from a good upbringing. That sounded good.

I just wondered if when my recovery was complete, I'd be stuck in a wardrobe by the Salvation Army.

"When are you going to quit?"
"Soon"

I never went anywhere. I didn't want to. And I was committed never to do anything out of guilt or obligation. So I did little or nothing. I guess I was mastering pure existence on some level, proving to myself that I had the right to exist and that I didn't have to earn or justify my existence by working, struggling, helping or pleasing. I had worked for years to gain the approval of others. No more! I had struggled for lifetimes, it seemed, to earn my own self-respect. No more! I would never do anything again that did not spring from the joy of my own aliveness, if such a thing existed.

I was a sedentary creature. Occasionally I would rebirth a client or trek to the living room to lead a little seminar about Creative Thought or Relationships. I was a Zombie.

At one point I gave myself the assignment not to get up in the morning until I could think of three exciting things to look forward to that day. Most days I couldn't come up with one. I stayed in bed for ages. I felt utterly useless, hopeless, and helpless. I wrestled with the angel of death, the sneaky little devil! I sank into self-pity. I wallowed in self-disgust. I stunk. (I didn't even shower.) I indulged in complete despair. I was not always fun to be with.

But all along I felt a certain process moving inside. Part of me loved the contradictions. I'd affirm to my subconscious mind: *The divine plan of my life now manifests.* My conscious mind would respond: *You asshole! The cosmic joke of your life now manifests!* And I'd envision myself a Bowery Bum or bagman, a homeless, hungry shell of a man, looking for shelter or soup to fill the empty pit in my gut.

I felt what it's like to be alone in an infinite universe. I could feel the solitude, the sorrow, even the self-pity which wants to romanticize alienation. Looking back at this period, I think it was one of the healthier things I went through. All my life I had avoided these feelings, covered them up, found comfort. Now I came to see that in any liberation process there is a stage where you pass through the illusion of utter aloneness. There is usually darkness, hopelessness, and futility just before a major breakthrough. I thought about the umbilical cord and the separation anxiety that resulted from its severing. Freedom always demands the loss of some attachment. And even though it is only dependency that is ultimately lost, the feeling of loss is nonetheless devastating.

My worst fear was that I'd be good for nothing. Whenever my parents were really angry with me, they'd call me a "good-for-nothing"! So somehow this thought represented the lowest of the low to me. It alone symbolized the threat of eternal banishment from the Garden of Eden. I could hear God's final judgement on me: *All in all, you were good for nothing! Go directly to Hell! Do not pass go!*

But during my self-imposed exile I came to see that being good-for-nothing was, in fact, not bad at all, and, indeed, a good place to start over again. It was a declaration of both my independence and my innocence. It was a statement that I was essentially good, and that I did not have to struggle to prove it. Moreover, settling into my innate goodness, I could relax and share it without anxiety, panic, or desperation. When I finally did go back to working full-time, it was with the certain knowledge that my love was good enough for me and everyone else, and that my love always did hit its target—no matter what the process looked like. I never again worried about my goodness. I had somehow overcome the basic moral dilemma!

I guess you could say that I gained confidence, certainty, or self-esteem. Whatever it was, I knew I would never again be the same.

All that time Mallie was a tower of strength, a pillar of patience and support. She would listen to all my fears, doubts, judgments, confusions, and she'd say, "Take your time. You're doing great." Or, "Relax. You're just in the middle of something!" Mallie had started rebirthing a year before me. She was the Sacajawea of my breath.

Receiving her love during those months when I was doing nothing was an amazing confrontation. At times, I just couldn't let it in. I hadn't done anything to earn it. I'd just push her away, or withdraw further into my process.

"I love you," she'd say.

"What do you mean by that?" I'd ask.

I'd look at her bright sunshiny face and literally have to cover my eyes. Her love was a blinding light to my ego.

I'd hide in paranoid fantasy, imagining that maybe Mallie had some ulterior motive beneath her love—maybe she was just warming me up as a prelude to some hideous crime she was concocting. I'd think of those Hitchcock movies—I'd do anything to test and sabotage. I became a royal pain in the ass.

I'd whine and complain; I'd argue and criticize. I'd get picky and mean and nasty and cruel. Someone once said that it's good to put your worst foot forward in a relationship. That way, if your partner can accept all your negative qualities, you don't have to worry about being rejected later, when they surface. Most people, of course, do the opposite. They hide what they don't like about themselves for fear of rejection should their partner discover these flaws. They select their most charming, seductive traits to reveal to others. Only trouble is, even if they suceed in winning love, they live in constant dread of the truth coming out. What you hide you end up hiding from!

And so I put my worst foot forward, secretly trying to trip up Mallie. In fact, I was hopping full steam ahead on my worst foot. Fortunately, she didn't "fall" for this one bit. Our sense of humor got the better of us again. I had a T-shirt that read *Angels fly high because they take themselves lightly.*

It became our motto.

"When are you going to quit?"
"Soon."

Our problems led to lessons, and our lessons became our teachings. We realized that every problem was once a solution to a previous problem. We both liked to fight, for instance. We each had a red belt in arguing. This had been the solution to (1) my growing up with a father who was both a defense attorney and Jewish, and (2) Mallie being born in the middle of four brothers who, well, boys will be boys.

So we fought at first. We could see we both thought loving meant fighting and that if you didn't fight you really didn't care. We also realized how addicted we were to being right.

As we became more enlightened, we had to acknowledge that since "what you think is what you get," one is always right in one's own mind. Each of us collects all the evidence we need to substantiate our particular point of view, anyway. Even diametrically opposed positions can be scientifically documented. So why fight?

So we evolved the thought: *I'd rather win love than arguments.* It became our *STOP-THE-BATTLE-CRY!* We created the Right Day Game. For 24 hours Mallie would be completely right, no matter what. I'd agree with everything she said. I remember one summer day I was hiding in the dark, looking for the womb or some such thing. Mallie always wanted to go to the beach and play in the sun. It was too much light for me. One day, *her* Right Day, we woke up and I looked out of the window.

"It's too cloudy for the beach," I said.

"It's sunny," Mallie responded.

"It's going to rain," I suggested.

"It's sunny."

"Thunder and lightning?"

"Sunny."

"Sunny?"

"Sunny!"

"Right. Sunny."

We went to the beach. It was the sunniest day of the year. The Right Day Game makes a joke of the whole issue of right and wrong. Also, it gives you an opportunity to experience how brilliant your partner often is—especially when you're not obsessed with defending yourself. Who cares who's right? If Mallie has the best idea, she is only too willing to share it with me. Letting her be right doubles my storehouse of intelligence, imagination, and intuition.

The more Mallie wins, the more I win. The more I win, the more Mallie wins. What's to fight about?

We created a joint affirmation—a thought to express all the qualities we wanted to expand in our relationship. We had a rule: If one of us started saying this affirmation aloud, the other was bound to join in. The affirmation is so long it is impossible to stay upset and repeat the whole thing. Our joint affirmation became another useful tool for circumventing dumb arguments. It goes like this: *Bob and Mallie always have and enjoy ever increasing love, health, happiness, wealth, wisdom, harmony, luxurious living spaces, easy and pleasurable travels and sexual bliss!* This thought uprooted my heart from many a potential depression.

I was such a cloudy person back then. I would look for the cloud wherever there was a silver lining. And if there wasn't a cloud to be found, I'd simply make one up. I remember flying to Barbados, looking out the window, seeing a white puffy thing in the middle of solid, endless blue and saying, "There's a storm brewing!"

Mallie brought the sun to me. Having grown up in Vermont, she had no patience with bad weather. This somehow carried over into our emotional life. I was a Jewish brooder. My basic cultural outlook was: "If there's a problem here, let's find it and make the most of it." Mallie's attitude was pure Vermont: "Let's get on with life!" If there was a problem, there was a solution. Life was simple. You took one step at a time. Right. Left. But I was still too busy hopping on my worst foot to be slowed down by mere walking. Besides, life without sulking seemed a depressing proposition. Suffering, struggle, guilt, angst—that was what life was about. Wasn't it?

God, how I loved my pain! In many ways I was more faithful to it than to Mallie!

There were times I knew I had to get rid of her while I still knew who I was. To surrender completely seemed like giving in, submission, loss of identity, death. At the same time, I had already decided she was the best thing in the world for me and that I would never leave her, come hell or high water—and they both came.

A relationship has a life cycle of its own. It seems to go through all the stages of growth from conception to birth to infancy to adolescence. And love has a death wish, too. I remember when it came up for us. It was like a tornado driving us. We were literally wrenched apart by an energy field so intense it seemed all we could do was circle the wagons or run for the hills.

Finally, we had an idea. We had to assert our will to love, to live, to survive together. We had to kill the death wish. So we created the 24 Hour Contact Game, which was the craziest dance we ever did—a physical contact sport which, in some ways, was more brutal than the Thrilla in Manila. For 24 hours we were glued together. We were touching every moment. We went everywhere together—the closet, the refrigerator, the bathroom, the supermarket, the telephone booth. Always in contact. Arm in arm, leg in leg, backs leaning on each other—always touching, always connected, entwined, limb over limb.

It was amazing. At times the energy pulling us apart was so powerful it would yank at us fiercely, like cross currents of wind. It was a tug of war. That night we went to a party. We drew people between us, bodies unconsciously attempting to break our hold on each other. It was a whirlwind. We spun and staggered, but we held firm and reasserted our grasp. The Force tore at us, but we had set our hearts on a course of action, and we would not relent. And then, finally, it died. It disappeared as suddenly as it had erupted, as if saying, "I see you have chosen to be together. I honor the strength of your bond."

The 24-Hour Contact Game was an emotional marathon that killed the beast of separation—or, at least, chased it off into the woods to lick its wounds.

> *"When are you going to quit?"*
> *"Soon."*

All this time I would see what a brilliant therapist, counselor, and healer Mallie was. She was astounding! Just her presence seemed to move mountains. And her wisdom was ancient, as her compassion ran deep. Plus she was an emotional telepath—and she usually knew what people were feeling before *they* did. She'd be in the kitchen, stirring a huge pot of her original pure Vermont spaghetti sauce (quite an accomplishment in itself) and a friend would walk in. She'd look perfectly normal to me, but Mallie would take a breath, lick some sauce off the wooden spoon and say, "What are you so sad about?" As if the whole world knew! In a flash, the person would dissolve in a puddle of tears, sobbing from her core, confessing her deepest feelings and darkest secrets. Mallie would calmly continue to stir the pot, reminding her "client" to breathe, joking and teasing her through it, and then inviting her to stay for some spaghetti. By the time our friend left she would have forgotten what she was healed of and be more concerned with the recipe for the spaghetti sauce.

There was never any fanfare about Mallie's intuitive powers. She never made herself special, always down-playing God's considerable gifts to her. When other spiritual teachers were around, Mallie would usually pretend she knew nothing, stirring her pot and taking everything in. I so admired her complete lack of ego, the purity of her love and desire to help people, and her invisible way of working on your soul.

I remembered what Lao-tse said about leadership in the 6th century BC:

> *A leader is best*
> *when people barely know he exists.*
> *Not so good*
> *when people obey and acclaim him.*
> *Worse when they despise him.*
>
> *But of a good leader*
> *who talks little*
> *when this work is done*
> *his aim fulfilled*
> *they will say:*
> *"We did it ourselves."*

Surely he was describing Mallie. Her ways were mysterious and often unspoken, but supremely effective.

I wanted very much for her to quit her job and work with me 24 hours a day. I wanted to play with her all the time, and work was as good an excuse as any to gain her full attention. I was becoming a rapid success in my self-improvement business. My heart was open; my mind fairly clear; and people were experiencing a lot of growth in my presence. Truthfully, it was often a mystery to me why. I never felt like I did anything special with anyone. I was just getting more comfortable being me, and the more I settled into who I was, the more people settled into being who they were in my presence. Then they'd call me a "clear channel," which I suppose means that you get good reception if you tune into me.

In any case I was moving ahead. The groups grew in size. We met in hotels instead of living rooms. I had to turn clients away, and train new rebirthers to handle all the business. Mallie became increasingly involved in the work, but she wouldn't let go of her nine-to-five job. It was her security blanket.

I came to understand how people create umbilical attachments to paychecks—however small they may be. The regularity is more significant than the amount. We crave some external source to nourish us, and we will worship that source 'til kingdom come—so long as it provides for us. Mother!

"When are you going to quit?"
"Soon."

I grew frustrated, impatient and irritable. I wanted all of Mallie all of the time. I felt it was our calling to be together, to work together. 24 hours a day! I knew Mallie felt it too. It was inevitable. You can postpone your purpose, but you must fulfill it. What was this delay?

As it turned out it was the perfect delay! Watching Mallie trot off to work every morning was slowly evoking the memory of my mother holding job and home together when I was a child. I came to forgive and appreciate my mother very deeply. I understood what an amazing juggler a mother can be. I remembered waiting eagerly for my mom to come home every day at 5:30. Then I let myself transfer this childlike excitement to Mallie—I allowed my love for my mother to shift to Mallie. It was a conscious transfer.

Very often people—independent people—are psychologically bound to their parents. These people tend to be functioning grown-ups rather than healthy adults. They need to sever the psychic cord that keeps the parent-child bond stuck in infancy. The child must one day realize he has matured physically, mentally, and emotionally to the point that he no longer needs his parents. At this point he frees himself to bond with a mature mate. But first he must let go!

Not being with Mallie 24 hours a day supported me in releasing my neurotic attachment to my mother, and by extension to all women. And it also aided me in letting go of all attachments, which, in turn, opened up space for greater intimacy with Mallie.

Waiting for Mallie, I let go of the part of me that had been waiting for women forever. I remembered once waiting for my sister for three hours on a subway platform. I remembered Saturday afternoons of my childhood, my dad and I waiting impatiently at Union Square for my mother to buy out Klein's bargain basement—now that's waiting! And I even re-experienced the waiting of my birth, when I had to wait for my mother to be ready, and she was waiting for the obstetrician to be ready.

So every day Mallie was rebirthing me from her office in Harlem, teaching me patience, persistence, perserverence, and love.

Soon the time came for Mallie to cut her cord, too. We had been together for six months. My income as a seminar leader, rebirther, and consultant seemed to be doubling every month—which didn't mean a whole lot when you consider where I started.

Still, Mallie's paycheck—regular, predictable, and enough to seem substantial—was for her, and by extension for me, the umbilical cord that was the source of our survival. We were definitely stuck in a survival consciousness. I remember even considering the consequences of her $100 per week unemployment check running out, six months after she actually did quit her job.

I was doing well. But I was self-employed, and there was no security in that. I was the Source, clearly, but there was no certainty in the future—at least not according to everything we had been taught.

Someone told me I was afraid of *real* success. I asked myself why. Why was I scared of having it all? The answer hit me from behind. It was my mother again. I remembered all the times she had said to me, "Bob, I'm only living to see you be a success!" I could see how, in my mind, my success would complete my mother's life and therefore kill her. This realization shook me to the core. I dialed my mother's number immediately.

"Mom?"

"Yes, Bob."

"Remember when you said you were only living to see me be successful?"

"Yes, I remember."

"Does that mean if I were rich you would die?"

"Don't be an idiot!"

"Well, that's what you said."

"That's not what I meant."

"Oh. Are you sure?"

"Sure I'm sure. If you don't believe me, test me!"

"I'll do that."

Who teaches you about life? Who teaches you about love and money, dreams and happiness? What is the recipe for success? How do you get life to give you what you want? There is no school, university, or institute that teaches you the formula for successful living. You live it the way you choose, learning as you go, making your mind up as you go, following your heart faithfully enough to find the things you look for and the things you love. There is no one path to take. There is no great traffic cop in the sky waiting to give you a ticket if you take a wrong turn. *There are no wrong turns.* You carve your path as you go, and where you end up is, somehow, where you've been going.

Mallie and I knew in our hearts that we would prosper by working together. Neither of us had ever imagined wanting to be with someone 24 hours a day, and here we were, desiring it so much it terrified us. We were happy with what we had, we didn't want to mess with it. It was clear to us we were each self-sufficient. We knew we didn't need each other. We were proven survivors. But somehow the thought of taking our hard-earned sense of self-made separation and diving together into a pool of common resources and complete interdependence seemed insane. I remembered being told as a child, "Never put all your eggs in one basket!"

I believe in diversification as much as all good investors. But I also know that in matters of the heart you must give your all to have it all. I'm not saying that you must work with your partner to be happy, but I am suggesting that if you are in love, sharing that love in a viable business form can be doubly rewarding. You can love your work a whole lot more if you love the people you're working with. (If you don't love them you can, at least, like them.) Of course, we were taught, ''Never do business with friends.'' And you don't want to bring that attitude into a business relationship with someone you love. We were also taught, ''Never take money from strangers.'' Well, if you can't take it from strangers, and you shouldn't take if from friends, who's left? Known enemies. And so, people tend to resent those who give them money—often their boss (who then becomes the target on which to project a tremendous amount of unconscious hostility about money and authority).

I always tell my students, ''It's doubly rewarding to do business with friends.''

"When are you going to quit."
"Soon."

And so we took the big leap! We formed our first business, Little Miracles, which soon became Only Miracles, which then became ISLP—International Seminars Leadership Programs. And we combined with Sondra Ray and Fred Lehrman to form Guided Productions, to promote the LRT—Loving Relationships Training. And we joined with Larry and Joan Tobin to form Open Heart Productions, to produce and distribute books and tapes.

Working with Mallie has been pure magic! Sometimes we feel like invisible angels, gently influencing the world for the better. Other times we feel like everyone's mom and dad, mirrors for people to clear their relationships with their parents, and, since whatever is unresolved with their parents affects their other relationships, thereby helping them to create their ideal relationships. And still other times it feels like we're monitoring God's construction gang.

If we can build the Bomb,
We can construct the Peace!

Mallie and I both have work in our blood. Sometimes it seems like we're workaholics. Sometimes we are. But usually we are loving what we do so much that it nourishes us more than it drains us. And it's fun. Mallie's father can't walk without a crutch. His hip is bad and he hobbles along. Yet he has a huge garden full of zucchini and peppers and carrots and the sweetest corn I've ever tasted. To see him overseeing his garden, on his knees weeding every plant, one by one, pulling himself along, is to see the work ethic at work—man tending the dominion God charged him with!

My mom has worked since she was 13. My dad, a lawyer, worked day and night. I remember him on the phone late at night, counseling clients seeking divorce, urging them to work it out, give it another chance, forgive each other. His heart usually got the better of his business sense.

Mallie and I made a business out of love. We brought Sondra Ray's Loving Relationships Training to New York, where we produced it for three years before learning to lead it. The LRT is a remarkable compression of enlightenment, psychology, spiritual wisdom, and common sense. Our association with it has been a constant reflection of our relationship, as well as one of our favorite ways of putting our relationship out into the world.

We also created several other trainings and workshops—The Completion Training, The Zen of Sex, The Stages of Growth, Love and Money. We developed our personal way of working, which we call Open Heart Therapy, and we began to combine our love of working together with our love of travel. Well, actually it was *my* love of travel at first. Mallie's roots made her a nester. I was the wild bird, the migrator. Getting Mallie to enjoy the road was as challenging as getting me to enjoy the nest. But in time we both enjoyed both—and the Bob and Mallie Show, as it were, became a successful touring show, too. We went throughout the states, Canada, Mexico, England, and now Israel, Australia and Greece. The more we worked around the world, the more the world became our home. We bought a home in Greece in 1983.

The more we made the world our home, the more the world flooded our home. Seekers from everywhere came to our little two-bedroom apartment on West 106th Street. Lonely souls, lost souls, angry souls, suffering souls—they all came to us for help. And we did what we could for everyone.

But our little home rapidly became inadequate for our needs. One night I was leading a seminar, and I realized I felt trapped in a corner, as if by 70 sandwiched sardines. Ironically enough I was discussing *NO EXIT TERROR.* I knew it was time to move.

When we moved into our brownstone, it seemed huge compared to our tiny apartment. Now we had three floors, a large kitchen and a huge cathedral-ceiling living room. It felt like a church. It seemed colossal. Then, within a few months, it too became a sardine can of compressed souls. "Oh well," we decided, "Earth is a family business, and everyone's come home."

We kept teaching our message, that Earth is family and all healing starts at home, that anything unresolved at home you take out onto the streets, to work, to every new relationship, to each new kiss and embrace. We talked about forgiveness and gratitude and acknowledgement and prayer. We moved people through rebellion and conformity, and supported people in expressing themselves as they were, not in reaction to others. We taught listening as opposed to responding, stillness as opposed to drama. We talked about self-respect, self-esteem, self-reliance, and self-surrender. We taught a combination of simple metaphysics, common sense, and intuitive know-how. Most of all we were willing to be there for people—we gave them the time and the space to fall apart and put themselves back together, to grow up inside, to find love or money or peace or happiness. We loved people as they were, and they tended to be enriched by themselves in our presence.

We loved loving. It opened our hearts more to have so many people reach out to us. But there were times we had to get away. When we bought the home in Mykonos, we thought we could finally be home alone together. Mykonos! A magical island for lovers. For the gods. The perfect romantic hideaway!

Or so we thought. But it didn't work out quite that way. People followed us. They flocked to our private paradise. Soon we were having business meetings and trainings in Greece. And the town of Mykonos recognized us and took us into its heart and its homes.

Finally we surrendered. We gave up all hope of anonymity. It's a small world, after all. And when we made it our home, the whole universe became our back yard.

We were in Mexico. We were leading the Advanced 7-Day LRT for 250 people. It was our wedding anniversary. We stepped out of the elevator and a mariachi band serenaded us with trumpets; 250 people cheered our relationship. We celebrated. Later, they sat us on the stage and all the trainers, friends, and business partners told stories about us. We were roasted with love.

I was trying to listen. I remembered a time early in our relationship. We were at Walton, New York, the old East Coast Training Center for rebirthers. It was late one night, and we had locked ourselves in our bedroom to escape the people we were already drawing to us for help. This was early in 1977. We had sneaked into bed at about 3 AM, and

I barricaded the door with a bookcase, which was the only way to keep people out. Or so I thought. We lay down on the bed, exhausted from the day's processes, and I expected us to fall asleep before we could say a word. But I was astonished, as I tended to be back then, that within a few minutes we were holding each other passionately, surrendering to the uncontrollable energy that swells up between us when it must. I was on top of Mallie, well inside her, when I heard the door move. I turned my head as the door opened about a foot, and Leonard Orr, the founder of Rebirthing, stuck his head in the room.

"Hi!" he said in his own inimitable way.

"Hi!" I said, fighting my embarrassment.

"Do you know when the next Money Seminar is in New York?"

"Why?"

"There's someone downstairs who wants to know."

"Can I tell him tomorrow?"

"He wants to know now." Leonard was a little devil.

"April 15!" I shouted at him, willing to say anything to get him out of the room.

"That's income tax day."

"I know."

"Thanks," Leonard smiled, shutting the door.

I turned my head back to Mallie, laughing underneath me. We both laughed 'til we finished. In Mexico, honored for our marriage by 250 supporters, that moment in Walton seemed more poignant than ever.

For Mallie and me, there was truly no escape.

Sometimes it's better to put your worst foot forward first. That way, if your partner accepts you, you'll know he or she loves you unconditionally. You will break the pattern of selectively revealing yourself, based on what you think will win people's approval. It's only when you're free to reveal your whole self in your relationships that you can experience true love.

It's doubly rewarding doing business with friends. In our culture we are taught that work and play, money and love are separate domains. This further reinforces the schizophrenia of living in a complicated world. And it's not true. If you think about it, it's far easier making money doing something you love than something you resent. First of all, you enjoy the work so much you have double motivation for doing it well—love and money. Second of all, your pleasure is so contagious, others will love to prosper you. Think about it: whom would you leave a greater tip, a waiter who hates serving you or one who enjoys it? Third of all, when you're doing what you love, you're doing your God-given purpose on this planet, and when you're on purpose you tend to have more success in life. The great tragedy of growing up is that parents and teachers often tell children they they have to give up their dreams and be "realistic" about their future in order to survive. So a potentially great musician becomes a computer programmer, or a child with a gift with words becomes an English teacher. And pretty soon everyone's creative imagination is submerged beneath their survival consciousness. Then you end up being a functioning grown-up instead of a healthy adult.

For two lovers to work together is a potentially wonderful experience. But first they must each be very clear. If there are any unspoken dependency issues which have not been handled, working together can become an emotional and financial drain. But once both people know with certainty that not only can they take care of themselves, but also each other, then forming such a partnership can be both incredibly lucrative and satisfying.

When you no longer need your partner in order to survive, then doing business together is based on a joint prosperity-consciousness that will serve both you and the world.

GETTING IN BED WITH MOM AND DAD

"Can I snuggle?"
"Why not?"

It must start at conception. There you are, one moment a glimmer in your father's eye, the next a living being in your mother's womb. In a flash you become a wedge between your mother and father.

Many parents report a sharp decline in sexual activity once they conceive a child. And if the decline is not immediate, it usually surfaces later in pregnancy, when the physical changes are greater. Often it seems as though the mother's energy has turned inwards, excluding her husband in favor of the unborn child. And dad's fear of causing mother and child harm results in his withdrawing his energy from his wife, thereby completing the origin of the incest triangle.

What does the unborn child make of all this? If, as I believe, this child is a highly sensitive, intelligent, telepathic being—receiving direct and subtle messages through its mother's emotional/neurological apparatus—what could he think? "I come between people I love," would certainly be one logical conclusion.

Pre-natal guilt is not out of the question!

When I was a baby, I had a terrible time at night. I would have nightmares, earaches and screaming fits, howling until my mother would swoop me off to bed, planting me squarely between her and Dad. I wonder what Dad was feeling. I wonder what Mom was feeling. For my part, I felt awkward lying between them. I sensed I was unwanted, a burden, an intrusion—loved, yes, but not entirely welcome.

Mom and I had a very special relationship. She would protect me from what seemed like a cold cruel world, and in return I would be a buffer between her and Dad. I don't think my experience was that unique. Ideally, mom and dad would be two self-sufficient people who agree to be mutually interdependent. Their bond would be so tight that when a child was born, he would easily receive the benefits of that bond. A sense of enough-ness would naturally flow from one generation to another. There would be no scarcity of love in either parent's mind and therefore the child would grow into a certainty of abundance. He would have no need to compete with mom for dad's attention, or with dad for mom's attention, because he would know that there was more than enough love to go around for everyone.

Would that it were always that way.

For most of us our parents came together not out of mutual self-sufficiency but in order to fill gaps in each other's lives. They needed each other. Their bond was symbiotic rather than collaborative. Then when a child comes along, usually he will bond with one of the parents more closely than they are bonded with each other. The result is that one of the parents ends up feeling left out, the way he or she felt as a child. In the final analysis, every child must grow up to the point where he is inevitably left out of his parents' relationship, at least sexually, but the strong energy bond between him and one of his parents will cause him to search for a suitable parental substitute as a mate. When he does mate with a partner, he may either find his sexual passion gradually diminish (the more he sets up his partner to be a parental substitute, the less he will be able to make love to her), or he may draw in a third party so he can feel like the child who ultimately was excluded from his parents' bedroom.

"Can I snuggle?"
"Why not?"

I think every child, at one time or another, has the fantasy of replacing his mother or father and doing a better job at being the husband or wife than the real parent. My version of this fantasy had an interesting twist.

I remember a recurrent dream I had as a child which crippled me emotionally for at least two years and which I never discussed with anyone until I was an adult. In the dream I shot and killed my father with his own gun. Then a man came to the door who looked exactly like my father. A double! He said we should hide the body in my dad's closet and that he would never reveal what had happened so long as I never revealed that he was an impostor. When I woke up I was in a cold sweat. I couldn't go near the closet for years and I would look at my father suspiciously, searching for some sign in his face—a wink, a gesture of some sort—to indicate the secret we shared. Even though I can now see the classical Oedipal nature of my dream, there is still an emotional part of me that thinks, "Maybe you did kill your old man."

I even remember one night when I was alone, waking up and sneaking to the closet—I was a teenager by then—and slowly opening the door. I smelled a mustiness I thought was death, and I could have sworn I saw the outline of my dad's body buried behind all his shoes in the back of the closet. It was so dark.

Talk about your skeletons in the closet!

Another experience which reinforced the incestuous nature of my early family relationships happened in the bathtub. My mother used to bathe me frequently, and I enjoyed it thoroughly. I'm sure it was the closest I ever got to being back in the womb. I remember the last time she ever bathed me. I was playing in the tub as usual. I guess I was five or six at the time. Mom was washing me down as usual. I was laughing as she cleaned my genitals, which was my favorite part of the deal—certainly far more pleasurable than washing my hair. I looked up at Mom and I could see what a wonderful time she was having. She looked at me, and she could see that I could see how excited she was. She suddenly grew embarrassed, made some excuse, and left the bathroom, never again bathing me.

I felt so guilty. What had I done to drive my mother away? I must have done something horribly wrong, but I couldn't for the life of me figure out what. Later in life, when women withdrew from me, I felt that same familiar mixture of guilt and innocence. The power of "the infant guilt syndrome," based on the thought that you always hurt the one you love (since you hurt your mother at birth) is a mighty thing!

If only parents would communicate to their children when they become uncomfortable with their sexual feelings. When a father tells his daughter not to sit on his lap any more, he is expressing a perfectly appropriate decision he has made. But the consequences of this decision can be devastating to the little girl, even if she isn't so little any more. She could conclude, "Since Dad didn't want me, I'm a failure as a woman and no man will ever want me!" Several years ago I noticed Kim, our oldest daughter, blossoming into a beautiful young lady. She was thirteen at the time. Her body was changing fast and for the better, in my opinion. I felt uncomfortable around my "incestuous" feeling, but couldn't take my eyes off her terrific body. I remembered my mother and when she stopped bathing me and how confusing the incident had been. So I called Kim aside, sat down with her and told her how attractive I found her and how uncomfortable I felt. She laughed. ''Oh, I know,'' she said, and that was that. Children know, but if their parents don't confirm the obvious, they tend to become confused about the consequences of living in an adult body.

When I felt physically rejected by my mother, I turned to my sister for solace. When I was born, she had developed a serious case of hives on her eyes. Clearly, she did not want to see the competition. So my presence not only drove a wedge between my parents, it separated my sister from the apparent source of her well-being. I think she always resented me for coming along and stealing the spotlight. Moreover, I was the male child, and there were certain advantages in that.

In time, however, we grew closer and closer, turning to each other for what we could not get from Mom and Dad. My sister is six years older than me, so she was always very capable of providing me with all the hugging and holding my mother no longer seemed comfortable giving to me. This seemed to be a viable substitute for a while. But then she went off to college and there was no one.

When I was thirteen, I was Bar Mitzvahed. I thought I was supposed to be a man then, so I began to look at girls differently. Somehow I now had God's permission to be macho. In my family, however, one learned very early not to get too close to strangers. At the same time, due to the internal emotional politics, I couldn't get too close to anyone at home. If I loved my mother too much, I seemed to alienate my dad. If I loved my dad too much, my mom would seem to get between us. And my sister had already left home and was keeping her private life a secret.

"Can I snuggle?"
"Why not?"

I guess I found the ''healthy'' middle-ground that most children settle for, holding my loneliness inside. So there I was in my pain at thirteen, a ''man,'' feeling separate from the people I was closest to, my family, and guilty for seeing girls as women for the first time. Whenever I looked at a girl in this new light, I felt in betrayal of my family. Yet I couldn't get what I wanted at home any more—was it love, affection, what? It seemed that growing up inevitably involved betraying the people I most loved.

I began to cloak my social life in secrecy, hiding my deepest desires as well as my actions from my parents. I remember trying to hide my first girlfriends from my mother. It was a futile gesture. My mother would spy on my activities, eavesdropping when I talked to a girlfriend or opening love letters addressed to me. I grew angrier and more surreptitious, learning how to be a secret agent sponsored by my sexuality.

Looking back, I can see that my mother was, in a sense, jealous, and that since her love and her possessiveness were so entangled, I was forced to rebel from both at the same time. I'm sure I concluded that if a woman really loved me she'd want to own me completely because I always re-created this pattern of looking outside my primary relationship until my partner would re-claim my attention with a jealous fit, proving to my subconscious mind that she, like my mom, loved me enough to get that upset.

Every upset is truly a set-up!

What is jealousy, anyway? According to the dictionary it is "intolerance of rivalry or unfaithfulness" and "apprehensiveness of the loss of another's exclusive devotion." According to me, it's a subconscious set-up to release all that primal pain, rage, and separation anxiety that we feel when we are born and the umbilical cord is cut, as well as when we discover that we're excluded from our parents' relationship in a fundamental way, as well as when we compete with our siblings for our parents' approval. Jealousy is a free purge from the universe. It's a socially acceptable way of going nuts. In some countries, even Texas I hear, you can kill a partner in a jealous fit and escape without punishment! These are called "crimes of passion" and I guess somehow they are deemed outside the realm of law and order.

There are three basic thoughts at the root of jealousy: (1) the Source of love is outside me; (2) there is a scarcity of love; and (3) therefore I have to conquer the Source of love and make it my own. This is probably an attempt to seize the reins of control in a relationship, and somehow balance the power that has gone too far in one partner's direction.

If you perceive love as coming from outside yourself and judge there to be a scarcity of that love, then every time your partner turns his attention elsewhere—be it to another woman, a football game, golf, his job—your primal panic can be activated. If your self-esteem is low, you tend automatically to create situations where people seem to take advantage of you. You will feel ripped off because you sell out to your partner, then feel controlled and manipulated by him. The outburst of a jealous fit could be your way of saying, "I've had enough of this . . . I deserve your undivided attention!" You might be saying this, but your statement is supported by all the rage for all the times you couldn't get that attention in the past. The Universe is so generous it gives you abundant opportunities to get out of need and into a sense of personal power and self-worth in your relationships.

If your incest case is severe enough, you might even attract a partner who is "married" to his work, football, golf, or long-distance travels. You will continually re-create the feeling of unavailability in order to release your longing for your father or mother, the first ones who were unavailable to you. Or you might fantasize about Mister Right or Miss Right, your soul mate or whatever, and use this image outside your relationship as a third party to draw energy away from your primary relationships. There are innumerable ways of creating incest triangles in relationships, and probably they all boil down to that yearning to climb back into bed, if not the womb, with mom or dad.

Several years ago I had a client who was in transition vis-a-vis relationships. He was in love with a wonderful woman, but his lady did not fit his picture of perfection. I gave him the following assignment: every morning when he woke up he was to cut out a picture of the most beautiful woman he could find in a magazine. Then he would bring it over to my house and burn it in the sink. He did this process for several months, during which time he came to see that the reality of his mate was far more lovely than any image he could find. Interestingly, at the same time he was doing all this, his partner was going through a physical transformation which greatly increased her beauty.

There is no one and only, no soul mate to withhold yourself for. Yes, you have one and only one mother and one and only one father, and the search for a perfect parental substitute can cause you to project this image onto your quest. This is counter-productive, however. Since your thoughts are creative, if you are looking for a relationship thinking there is only one right person out there for you, you will be searching for a needle of perfection in a haystack of humanity. And if you do find a wonderful relationship, your mind's addiction to Mister Right or Miss Right will cause you to wonder whether you're with the right one and to withhold yourself from surrendering fully to any one person because he or she might not be the right one. You might develop the attitude of *I'll wait and see if this one is right and if it is, I'll surrender fully to it.*

Of course, this never works because until you give your all, how can you have it all? Until you give your heart away, you're just saving it for someone else.

"Can I snuggle?"
"Why not?"

When I met Mallie, all my searching flew out the window. I knew right away that she was the one I wanted to make my one and only and that I would give up anything to have it so. Sex was so fabulous between us that it seemed we had both been virgins on some level until we made love. When we would touch each other, every cell in both our bodies seemed to wake up and embrace. We couldn't stop breathing together. We kept surrendering to deeper and deeper levels which took us to greater and greater heights. When one cycle of making love seemed to be complete, it simply served as the launching pad for an even more passionate journey to bliss. It was so powerful, gentle, tender, safe—it blew us away.

I never thought our sex life could get any better, but I have always been surprised at how much better it always gets.

Our relationship was so good so fast—and not just sexually—that our need to sabotage it was activated before we knew what was happening. The closer I got to Mallie, the more I would go on automatic, and look outside the relationship, thereby turning secretive and creating a private life separate from her. What was I looking for? Nothing. I had exactly what I wanted so what else was there? It was simply my family pattern of thinking I couldn't have it all with anyone who loved me so much. I was addicted to separating myself from love, then looking for it outside myself.

Mallie's pattern dovetailed with mine. She came to remember that when she was an infant, she slept in her mom and dad's room. She would be asleep in her crib and then wake up from the sounds of her mom and dad making love. She would pick herself up and lean over the crib, fascinated by how much fun her parents were having. "Whoopie!" was her thought. She got off on watching. As an adult, she unconsciously pulled in other women, often good friends of hers, and then left herself excluded from my love for them. Her reaction as an adult, however, was not exactly "Whoopie!"

What we wanted was what Mallie calls "Monogamy From The Heart"—a space where we both felt free and in that freedom chose to embrace monogamy whole-heartedly because that choice represented greater ease, pleasure, and nourishment to our souls.

Part of my addiction to "other women" was based on my jealousy towards Mallie's children. On the one hand I was angry that she had such a wonderful bond and that I had never had that as a child. On the other hand, I was simply jealous that she had children and I didn't. At first I used my position as "intruder," lover, and stepfather as an excuse to stay separate from the children. I would compete with them for Mallie's undivided attention. I'm sure I acted just like my dad, even though he was my real dad and I was a surrogate father. When I realized this, I had to admit that my behavior probably would have been exactly the same had I been the children's legitimate father.

Still, my illegitmacy as a father helped support my illegitimacy as a husband and further sponsored my pattern of sneaking around.

My childhood had been further complicated by my never having my own room. I learned how to sleep around early in life. We had two bedrooms. One was my parents' and one was my sister's. In the course of my childhood I was shuffled around from room to room. I slept in my parents' room, my sister's room, shared a room with my mom, then my dad, then slept in the living room before finally getting my sister's room when she moved off to college. I was a wandering Jew even in my own home.

I think that being Jewish heightened my sense of secrecy—somewhere in my mind was a fear that I had to hide to survive. This fed my general paranoia that was based on the thought from birth: *People are out to get me!*

The closer I got to Mallie, the more my suspicious nature would be activated. I would think: *She's not even Jewish.* But of course she was. She had converted to Judaism before her first marriage, and she knew more Jewish history, culture, and Yiddish than I did. Still, she didn't have Jewish blood, and I held this against her.

It was ironic. Mallie never gave me one good reason to mistrust her while I gave her every reason. Yet in the end our mistrust was equal. What it came down to was that neither one of us trusted ourselves enough to be certain we wouldn't betray ourselves again. We looked for some new faith to pull us through.

"Can I snuggle?"
"Why not?"

I can now see that we all tend to be addicted to lack of intimacy. Whenever we are confronted with being closer to a lover than we ever were to any member of our family, we tend to slam on the brakes, make a U-turn and head in the opposite direction. We'd rather divide ourselves in fragments and share a piece here and a piece there than surrender fully to one love.

Why would we do this if we were not already fragmented? When we are schizophrenic in our behavior, it shows us what we have denied ourselves within and gives us an opportunity to nourish that piece of us and bring it back into the fold.·

The intimacy threshhold tends to stay stuck at the same points we felt affection withdrawn from us as children.

Mallie and I eventually got through all of this. We sat down and told each other everything. We shared our complete sexual histories with each other, our fantasies, our judgments, and our mistrust. We learned to trust our mistrust by accepting it, until it brought us into a greater trust. We did meditations where we ''uncorded'' all the energy cords from previous relationships. We wrote letters of completion with anyone who might remain in the way of our being together. We did 24-hour-contact days. We chose our relationship daily. We prayed a lot. We did everything in our power to complete our perfect bond. And in the end, our desire to surrender proved greater than our fear of loss, and we yielded to the holiness of being united together.

The power of a pattern is nuclear in scope. Since a pattern is unconscious repetitive behavior, becoming conscious of it is the first step out. Noticing the level of addiction to the pattern is the second step. The third is choosing out of it. Choosing out of a form of behavior that has been part of one's personality since conception is not always easy.

It requires tremendous persistence, patience, purpose, and prayer.

But finally it is so simple. You say *no* to what you don't want and *yes* to what you do want and it all works out. Even when an old pattern, such as incestuous energy, tempts with all its seductive strength . . . even when you are attracted to the point where every cell of your body wants you to say *yes* to what your mind and heart no longer want . . . you simply take a breath, say no thank you, and continue on your merry way.

Yes, it's scary. It's always frightening to let go of what's familiar—even if you hate it—and dive into the unknown. But if the love that you're looking for is something you have never known, you can only create it in unknown territory. And God always seems to fill a void with something better than what you had before.

Once you release the pain of the past, once both partners have established equal power that coexists harmoniously in one relationship, once you have overcome separation in your partnership, then, theoretically, you would never again set up triangles, physical or psychic, in your love life. For me, however, the ugly creature reared its head one last time after I thought I had released it forever, and it did so at a moment when I was least prepared to deal with it. This time, Mallie was beyond jealousy, and the hurt was real and present-time.

I looked at her hurt and I could feel it in my body. I think it was the first time I experienced the hurt I caused my partner as the hurt I caused myself. Since we had become so much a part of each other, it was no longer possible to hide in my separation and pretend the pain was outside myself. Why would I want to hurt someone I loved so very much, I asked myself. Why? It just didn't make sense. It could only be that Mallie's immense love for me represented some terrible threat to a part of myself I was too scared to look at . . . the part that had defined my power by choosing to be separate and alone, the part that wouldn't surrender 100%, the part that would die before it let anyone touch me that deep again. It was that last separate piece I had to release to know that Mallie and I would make it forever.

One thing I learned for sure. Love based on secrecy is love trying to hide from itself.

I recently divulged a financial secret to Mallie. I had been saving a secret stash of hundred dollar bills. I had several thousand dollars hidden in an old wallet in a drawer full of socks. In thinking about my secret stash, I realized it was the same pattern. I saw that part of me was saving this money for myself, should Mallie and I ever separate.

My secret stash was my investment in separation. I felt so much release in sharing this with Mallie (the secret as well as the money) that I now feel empowered to tell her everything. It enabled me to feel my heart's strong desire to pool all of me with all of Mallie.

Another time I was trying to hide a thought from Mallie. After six months of living together I was overwhelmed with feelings of love for her. But, in the middle of it all, one thought disturbed me: "I need her." For weeks I kept it to myself. It was the last thought I wanted to reveal. Need was unmanly, unromantic, and unenlightened. Still, it was what I was feeling and I was trying to deny it. Suddenly, one day, I blurted it out in the kitchen. "Mallie, I need you." She turned around and smiled at me. "I know," she replied. "I need you, too."

She knew. Love always seems to know it all.

You can't hide from people who love you that deeply. Love is a bright light which shines on every corner of your being. You can try to hide in the shadows temporarily, but it is a futile gesture. In love even your darkest thoughts are touched by the light.

Mallie is much like my mother in this respect: the power of her love and intuition opens me up more than I often care to acknowledge. Quite frankly, she is the most powerful woman I have ever met, and I've stumbled across quite a few in my day. Mallie can see things in me (and others) that I have not yet seen in myself, let alone shown. Her eyes beam like lasers into the deepest corners of my being. She feels what I feel in my body, even when I don't want to acknowledge feeling it. There is no way I can ever hide the essence of anything from her. And at last I can say, *thank God!* I am certain one of the main reasons I drew her to me was to learn that it is safe to reveal everything. And that it is safe to let a woman love me fully.

"Can I snuggle?"

Mallie and I were sleeping. Kim's voice woke us up. She had had a nightmare and wanted to crawl in bed with us.

"Why not?" replied Mallie, and Kim slithered between us. We both held her for a few minutes. There was no separation, intrusion, or awkwardness in any of our bodies. After a few minutes, Kim got up and went down to her room to sleep.

"I love you," I whispered to Mallie.

"I love you," she whispered back. We hugged.

In the end, the love that you make is truly equal to the love that you take.

Since your first experience of relationship is mom, dad, and you, you tend to grow up and think of your relationships in threes. Since your thoughts are creative, triangles become commonplace in most relationships. Sometimes the third party is a person. Other times it's your partner's job, hobby, even the TV or newspaper. Still other times it can be a fantasy, an image of perfection you use to withhold yourself from the one you're with. It can be anything. People are in the habit of feeling divided energetically between two forms, probably representing mom and dad.

The only "one and only" is the one you choose to make your one and only. Once you make this choice, any thoughts that come between you and your total bonding with a mate are likely to come up for healing. You may find yourself attracted to other people, even when you are totally satisfied with your mate. You may draw in a third party for your mate to be attracted to, just to heal your "incest case." There are many techniques for handling these situations which are discussed in Part Two of this book. But in the final analysis it all comes down to choice—in choosing to surrender to one relationship fully you inevitably go beyond yourself in a relationship, perhaps beyond the "intimacy threshhold" established in your family. You enter unknown territory, which, though scary, is the perfect place in which to create a relationship more wonderful than you have ever known before.

Your mind gravitates towards the familiar. Your heart wants what it has never felt before—it drives you on, beyond all familiar signs until you reach one that reads, "Proceed without caution!" Then you know you're on the right path.

And finally you learn, contrary to what you are taught, that it is not only safe to put all your eggs in one basket, but in doing so you are creating a truly abundant nest!

THREE IS A CHARM

"A difference marriage would make is . . . well, I'd be trapped forever."
"Thank you!"

Mallie and I were together for four years before we ever broached the subject of marriage. Mallie had been married once for 14 years and I had been married twice for a total of nine years. You would think that with 23 years of marital experience under our belts, we would have accumulated some wisdom on the subject. Not so! We knew more about quantum physics than about marriage, and we knew absolutely nothing about quantum physics.

My first marriage was very much like the completion of my Bar Mitzvah. It was just another futile gesture to express this ineffable quality called manhood. It turned out that I had not really attained this state at 13 so I got another chance at 22. Even the wedding ceremony felt like my Bar Mitzvah, down to the accordionist in the band and the chicken on the plates. At both celebrations I remember thinking, "Is this for me or my family?" Even as I shattered the glass I wondered if I was 13 or 22. Had I grown up, or just grown?

The main difference between the two occasions was vis-a-vis girls. When I was Bar Mitzvahed, I was somewhat relieved to say good night to my girlfriend and go home with my parents. When I was married, I was not at all relieved to say good night to my parents and go upstairs to the honeymoon suite and be with a wife—my wife. I felt just as awkward at 22 with my wife as I had at 13 with my girlfriend. I remember sitting on a king-size bed after the wedding. My wife was crying uncontrollably, and I couldn't imagine why. I felt utterly helpless, unprepared, and immature, all of which I indeed was. All I could say was, "Should I order a pizza?"

My mother had taken me aside a week before the wedding. She was finally going to teach me the missing ingredient in the recipe for successful living. "Bob," she said, "I have something to tell you. I was married once before. When I was 22. To a gambler." *God, I thought, What is she telling me and why now? Am I gambling by getting married? Am I doomed to divorce because I'm 22 too? Is that the message? Or maybe I'm illegitimate, or my real father was the gambler and he's the skeleton in the closet. Or maybe she's being more symbolic and referring to the Great Gambler in the Sky who rolls the dice of our lives?* My mind was racing. "Don't tell your father I told you," she whispered. "He made me promise not to tell anyone."

More secret diplomacy!

The day of the actual wedding, shortly before the ceremony, my dad pulled me aside to offer me some advice, or so he said. Was he finally going to tell me the facts of life? Did he think I was still a virgin? "Bob," he said, patting my back, "I want to tell you about marriage . . . ." He puffed on his cigar, a regular George Burns. "Always . . . *always* take care of the lady." He whispered in my ear, "Be gentle" . . . . *Is that it?* I thought, *Be gentle . . . a scholar and a gentleman . . . .* I was ready!

"A difference marriage would make is . . . it would make our relationship boring forever."
"Thank you!"

My first wife, Elizabeth, was the girl of my parents' dreams. She was Jewish. She came from a wealthy family that owned a country home in the Hamptons and a city home on Madison Avenue. Her stepfather was a renowned cardiac surgeon. She was well-educated, a graduate of Barnard College just like my sister. She was pretty, witty, and the quintessential Jewish American Princess. What more could any parent want for his Jewish American Prince? What more could I do to please Mom and Dad than lay my heart at the foot of a woman who was certain that her way was God's way and, if not, God would surely defer to her? Surely, I would now find happiness. Surely, I had finally made it.

Fat chance!

I must have been crazy back then. I can hardly relate to the person-I-was-then as me, and were it not for the fact that I'm sure I will some day look at myself as I am today and feel equally superior, I would just as soon bury the me-I-was-then in the back of that closet with my dad.

In fact, my relationship with Liz had begun the year I was Bar Mitzvahed. I had met her at summer camp in North Carolina. High Valley! The camp had been my first ticket away from home, and the freedom, fun, and friendship I experienced stayed in my heart forever as cherished memories. I didn't, however, cherish the memory of Liz at High Valley. She was in love with another boy, Kenny Rigler, who was older, taller, and a far better athlete than I. I didn't even bother to compete.

It was six years later that I again bumped into Liz. I was a senior at Columbia College and she was a sophomore at Barnard. I was walking down Broadway when I suddenly got walloped by a girl's handbag. I looked up and it was Liz. Maybe I should have known better. When a handbag hits your head, maybe you should draw certain obvious conclusions about the nature of the relationship. But when I looked up at her, I knew nothing. I fell in love, or at least that adolescent crush that Kenny Rigler had so rudely interrupted was re-awakened in my gut, like a fire that needed to burn itself out.

Truly, I am grateful for all I learned with Liz, even though I didn't learn what I had learned until it was too late. I remember meeting her for a drink about a year after we divorced. We were sitting opposite each other, speechless, at the Copper Kettle on West 72nd Street. It was one of those poignant, senseless scenes from a Woody Allen film. We sat and stared at each other like complete strangers. As I looked at her I remembered meeting her at High Valley Camp in North Carolina. I relived my jealousy over Kenny Rigler. "What went wrong?" she asked me. "I don't know," I answered. "Neither do I," she replied. And that was as complete as we ever got. Our ignorance about what went wrong seemed to be the one thing we could agree on. I think it freed us in some mysterious way.

Looking back, it feels like a dream more than a reality. Maybe that's just a function of how much I had to detach in order to survive the pain. Or maybe I was just too in love with the fantasy ever to experience the reality. Whatever!

"A difference marriage would make is . . . well, it could ruin our sex life."
"Thank you!"

What does it really mean to fall in love? And why would anyone want to fall into anything, let alone love? When I think of falling for someone, I think of that sinking feeling in my gut, I think of original sin or the fall from grace, when Adam fell for Eve who had fallen for the serpent who tempted her into thinking she was less than she was. When I fall for something, or someone, it is always because I am naive. Love is blind to the extent that you fall for it. Fools fall. Wise men rise in love.

To fall for someone is to sink into your lower self, and then expect your partner to be your higher self and pull you out of the muck. Usually, you're trying to pull him into the muck while he's trying to pull you out, and the result is a stalemate, if you'll pardon the pun.

I fell in love with Liz, went unconscious, only to wake up three years later to discover I wasn't in love at all, I was in trouble! At the time of our marriage, I think I suffered from a popular misconception of what marriage is, or can be. I thought that when you got married, it was a ticket to the future, a promise of what was to come. I thought that a wedding was a magical ritual which would automatically transform an ordinary relationship into an extraordinary one. In practical terms, I thought marriage would give me a security I hadn't found within. I'm sure I felt that marriage was a free pass to all the love I ever wanted forever. I guess I thought that God guaranteed every marriage. How or why I had these thoughts is beyond my understanding. Perhaps one possible explanation is that, at the time, I was dumb!

Now I view marriage quite differently. I see it as an expression of what is, not a promise of what will be. When Mallie and I started marrying others, we immediately saw that a wedding was simply the public acknowledgement of a union that had already occurred. To be joined in holy matrimony is to reveal to the world the depth of your devotion and the height of your love. This concept of marriage is really nothing new or radical. In fact, it is more in line with the sacred bond marriage was always supposed to be. During the Industrial Era, however, with the rise of the middle class (and the legal establishment), marriage was reduced to a social contract, a convenient means of establishing ownership and arranging for the smooth transference of material possessions upon death. People tended to forget about spiritual union, relegating it to romantic novels, and possession replaced surrender as the primary motive for being with someone. Nowadays, more and more couples are reasserting the spiritual essence of marriage, looking for a kindred spirit as well as a compatible partner.

"A difference marriage would make is . . . I'd have to take care of someone else and I can barely handle myself."
"Thank you!"

In my first marriage I acted out the dream of bourgeois marriage, imitating an empty form which in itself was a cheap copy of a holy sacrament. Yet I am completely grateful for the experience. My first marriage was perfect for me at the time. It gave me a bridge to cross, and when I had crossed it I could look back and see my family waving. I could both leave and stay connected to those I love. Liz was the perfect mirror in which I could see both my strengths and shortcomings. She was a strong, grounded woman, and her support made my days in graduate school less heady and more hearty than they might otherwise have been. She helped give me the courage to endure my first professional teaching job, as an English instructor at Cleveland State University. We headed for the midwest and learned we could, indeed, survive away from our parents and make it on our own, if we wanted. Liz always supported me in going for what I really desired in life, and so we headed back east after a year, to Yale University, where I could pursue playwrighting at the drama school and she could go for her Ph.D. in French.

The more we succeeded in our careers, the more our relationship seemed to suffer. Looking back, I can see that my Primal Law (lowest thought about myself) had to manifest itself somewhere. And since everything else was more than good enough, I subconsciously chose Liz to fail at. I withdrew from her, withheld from her, and resented her for not reading my mind and giving me what I never had the courage to ask for.

I was a coward at home and a local hero in the world. The last year of our marriage I was obsessed with Vietnam, organizing the draft resistance movement in New Haven. I drove down south for Martin Luther King's funeral. I marched on the Pentagon. I thought about renouncing my U.S. citizenship in protest and spending the rest of my days in Sweden or England or Canada. Needless to say, this would put any wife to the test, let alone one who had bargained for middle class values. I'm sure there was a part of Liz using me to get back at her parents, especially her disapproving stepfather whom she resented. Nevertheless, she was amazing in her support for my decisions, and even when it was clear that our stars were rapidly becoming uncrossed, Liz stood behind my political positions loyally.

I was a rebel. My revolutionary postures were obvious expressions of my desire to overthrow my father, not my country. You could have shown me any good authority and I would have given you ten good reasons to remove him from the face of the earth.

When you are a revolutionary at heart, you are deeply committed to doing things differently from your dad. Marriage becomes one of those vestigial institutions from a bygone era. Of course it must come tumbling down.

I didn't want to be associated with any parental structure. I was an anarchist seeking formlessness in which to discover my own internal order. I was burning bridges, not building them. Of course I had to get divorced. It was the ethical thing to do!

Now I know that a relationship not devoted to a higher purpose is doomed to fail. Liz and I got married in order to get married. We never thought there was more to it than that. We came together to handle our insecurities, and so the big questions of our time together were where to live, what jobs to take, what car to have, what kinds of food to eat. This is not the stuff of happiness! In trying to settle down, we kept looking at settling for less than who we were and something inside each of us said no and so we split up.

She was looking for me to make her whole, and I was looking for her to make me whole. There was never a strong common purpose in being together. We were married, not because each of us was following his heart's desires and that led to the same path, but, rather, because we thought if we took the path most frequently travelled we would somehow find our hearts' desires along the way. It doesn't work that way, my friend.

No wonder we felt so awkward. We were like children acting like our parents . . . kids trying to walk in our parents' shoes. We stumbled and fell . . . out of love.

"A difference marriage would make is . . . you have to live in the suburbs."
"Thank you!"

You have to become your own perfect partner before you find someone else to fill those shoes. You have to be happily yourself before you can be happily married. You have to be a responsible human being, which is different from being laden with responsibilities. You have to have a personal relationship with God, which is different from being religious. You have to have a purpose in life. You have to love love. You have to feel the advantage of sharing. You have to grow up.

I don't believe in soul mates. I don't believe there's any one-and-only, Mister Right, or knight-in-shining-armor to sweep you off. There are many fish in the sea, many baits, many hooks, and in the end the loving, for most people, is in the fishing, not the catching. The only one-and-only is good old mom or dad, and one thing is for certain: you can't have either one of them!

It was my birthday, 1969. I was flat on my back with the flu at Yale University Infirmary. It was Christmas vacation and the whole student body had pretty much gone home. I was 26 years old, all alone, sniffling, feeling good and sorry for myself. It was my coldest Christmas.

I wondered if I'd ever get married again. I felt so ashamed and humiliated. I had failed at life's most basic game, relationships. I was empty at my core. I had no idea who I was or what I wanted to do with my life. And what was worse, I was bored stiff.

I kept thinking, "It's better to have loved and lost than never to have loved at all." That sounded fine, comforting even, but when you're totally lost, you wonder if you ever loved at all, and if you didn't, what it is you're so sad at having lost? Basically, I cried a lot and didn't know why. Looking back, I'd have to say I released a lot of old hurt. At the time, it felt utterly hopeless.

Two years later when I met my second wife Kathy, I was writing plays and riding an emotional high. I lived in Greenwich Village, worked days at Kings County Hospital to pay the rent, and wrote all night. I had spent some time in London as a playwright-in-residence for a young English theatre company. I guess I was more determined than ever to get my drama out of my head and onto the stage.

At Kings County Hospital I worked for the Department of Social Services, interviewing people in the psychiatric ward to see if they were eligible for Medicaid. There was one patient I remember in particular, John Knowitall. The first time I interviewed him, he told me his name, and I laughed. But he was serious. The second time I interviewed him, he told me his name was Moses and he was a mountain climber.

I began to write a play about this man. It was called *California Jubilee,* about a conspiracy to kidnap a madman from Kings County and relocate him to California, where no one would notice. I had travelled to Europe and the Caribbean, but never out West. My heart was yearn-ing for wide open spaces. It was in this context that I met Kathy, a Califor-nia girl.

Kathy was clearly a kindred spirit, but hardly a compatible part-ner. Everything was perfect in our relationship except for all the prac-tical details that make for survival, things like money, a home, jobs, and so on. We never could get it together to get it together, but the roller coaster we took was one helluva ride.

Kathy was an actress and our paths had crossed in drama school, but our stars had to wait a couple of years. I met her walking out of a play. We walked. We talked. There was an air of availability about us. I asked her out. She said yes. Time stopped. We made love as the heat of summer descended. It was Italian Unity week. It was July 4th. Inde-pendence was exploding all around us. The fireworks were just beginning.

That summer we drove cross-country three times. We left New York after my sister's wedding. It was 3 AM and we drove all the way to Niagara Falls, then headed west across Canada. That was the summer I awakened to the beauty of America. I saw the Great Lakes and the Great Plains, Banff and Lake Louise, Puget Sound and the Cascade Mountains, the Great Redwoods and the Golden Gate. By the time we pulled into San Francisco, our heads were really spinning. We seemed addicted to seeking, usually at the expense of finding. Our spirits were too restless to stop. We got back in the car and steered south for the Mo-jave Desert, where I was totally blown away by the magnitude of Death Valley, the Hopi Indian Reservation—where I could have stayed for-ever—and the City of Three Cultures, Santa Fe, where we got married.

I think we really got married just to drop anchor. I remember sitting on a park bench, trying to decide. Should we or shouldn't we? It was much like trying to figure out what direction to drive next when you have nowhere to go. We might have even flipped a coin. We were either grasping at straws or looking for divine intervention. Something to stop the whirlwind we felt bound by.

The wedding was nothing like a Bar Mitzvah. We discovered a renegade Catholic priest to marry us. Father George ran a home for way-ward children—many of the California flower children ended up home-less in Santa Fe, trail's end to be sure! The ceremony was small, incredibly spiritual, and held in a friend's back yard. I remember a long moment of silence in the middle, and then jet fighters from a nearby base roared overhead. I thought of the Hopi, the people of peace, and Los Alamos, where they made atomic weaponry, and wondered what the significance of being married so close to war and peace was. After the ceremony, I noticed I didn't feel any better nor clearer about where to go or what to do with my life. Kathy looked at me, expecting some sort of guidance now that we were married. "Let's keep driving," I said.

> *"A difference marriage would make is . . . well, it's expensive."*
> *"Thank you!"*

Kathy and I were romantic lovers, rebels, unfit for the real world. We never had any money, careers, or a roof of our own. We seemed to keep all the normal things of life away from us. It was as if there was something in the nature of our relationship that was opposed to life itself. We resented having to deal with survival issues. I guess you could say we just didn't want to grow up.

Like Romeo and Juliet and all the great romantic lovers, we were separate everywhere we went. We had taken our individual feelings of separation and tied them into one big separate knot. It was a case of "you and me, babe, against the world." The only problem was the world kept on winning.

The craziest times were the days of *Kopavi*. I had written a screenplay called *Kopavi*, the Hopi word meaning "the door at the top of the head." It was a comic romantic adventure and I almost succeeded in selling it to a major company. However, at the last minute I decided to make it with a group of friends. So began the days of *Kopavi*. We lived communally, Kathy and I often rolling out a foam rubber mattress and sleeping under a counter. We all had a lot of nothing, but we had this dream of filming our cross-country chase film together. The weeks passed into months, the months into years. Nothing was happening. No money was forthcoming. I was stubbornly clinging to a dumb fantasy. It was a wedge between us.

We had some heavy battles. Some she won; some I won. But we both lost the war. What were we fighting for? I can now see that we were rarely upset for the reason we thought. Mostly I think we fought—and people fight—because we wanted to surrender. It's an old cliche that first you fight, then you make up. And I think this is the unenlightened way people tend to go about their relationships. In the desire to fight is the drive to break down the wall of separation. In the making up is a temporary release from the wall. But no amount of fighting can really topple a wall that exists in the mind. Since what we believe in our hearts is what we get in our lives, so long as we believe we need walls to survive we will continue to construct these subconscious barriers to love. That's what happened to Kathy and me. On the one hand was this deep love and consequential desire to surrender; on the other hand was this basic mistrust that we would always be there for each other. Kathy's father had died when she was young, and I didn't trust women at all. I knew they were out to get me. Because we loved each other so much, we activated our worst fears. Unfortunately, we were not wise enough to free ourselves of those fears without freeing ourselves of each other.

"A difference marriage would make is . . . well, it makes leaving harder."
"Thank you!"

When you fall in love with someone, you instantly recognize an eternal connection, a timeless oneness. There is no logical explanation for how you feel since you have only just met the person and have no human scale capable of measuring the depth of your love. Yet you know this person. In your heart you have known him forever; in your mind you have only just met. The mind can never measure the eternality of the heart, and to the heart the mind's measurements are entirely insignificant. That is why love is so schizophrenic. On the one hand it is forever, while, on the other hand, it is doomed to pass.

So what do you do? What I did with Kathy was try to box the eternal into a practical lifestyle. It never worked. I could never bring the two worlds together. My deepest desire was to bring the practical up to the level of the eternal, but I just didn't know how to do it. The more I chose one world, the more I lost the other. Until I finally lost both worlds.

In 1974 Kathy and I took the EST Training together. At the time I was the director of theater arts at a Quaker boarding school in Bucks County, Pennsylvania, while Kathy was going for her master's degree in dance therapy at Temple University. Between the two weekend workshops, our 100-year-old Victorian house burned to the ground. We were out for dinner that night. My new typewriter, with my new play in the drum, was struck by lightning. This somehow symbolized the impossibility of having a career and a home at the same time.

I was standing on the lawn, watching the flames soar a hundred feet into the air. The firemen were doing all they could, which wasn't

much. A reporter from a local newspaper was asking me, "How does
it feel to watch all your possessions go up in smoke?" What a dumb
question. I couldn't even begin to answer. We had no insurance. What
was lost, including several original manuscripts, was up in smoke forever. Yet, deep in my heart, I felt incredibly free, unburdened of the
trappings of a lifestyle I never wanted. Moreover, I felt alive, and gratefully
so. My mind, body, and spirit were all in perfect working order. I could
see that everything burning had no lasting value. I let it all go. I had
what counted!

Six months later I won a playwrighting contest. My play, *Sand
Dwarfs,* won a National Endowment for the Arts grant to be produced
by Theater Arts Corporation of New Mexico. So it was off to the City
of Three Cultures, Santa Fe, again—the birthplace of our marriage and,
soon to be, its burial ground. We lived there one more year. Kathy worked
in a health club while I directed *Jesse and the Bandit Queen,* which somehow
summed up all the futility and frustration I was feeling regarding relationships. It all came to a head during Fiesta week in September. In Santa
Fe they electrocute a huge puppet, *Zozobra,* the god of gloom, every Fiesta.
Watching that puppet burn was like watching my house burn, only now
it was my inner possessions that seemed to go up in smoke—though the
final act of separation was still several months off. I soon left for New
York to see if I could land any directing work. The day I left, our little
white kitten Egg was hit by a truck and managed to drag its bloody body
to the middle of our king-sized white bedspread, where she died. I cried
more over the kitten than the marriage.

> *"A difference marriage would make is . . . we'd have to agree on what kind
of car to buy."*
> *"Thank you!"*

After we divorced, Kathy and I had dinner together. It was one
of those fine California restaurants. It was not like a Woody Allen movie.
More like a Hollywood set, which seemed appropriate. I had a couple
of drinks and turned quite emotional. Maybe it was the first time in my
life I really poured my heart out to another person. I shared all my hurt,
resentment, and guilt—it all came tumbling down. When I was done,
we just looked at each other, as in love as ever, but with our path together clearly behind us. "What went wrong?" Kathy asked. "We loved
each other, still do," I said, "but marriage was the wrong package!"

I never planned to marry again. I alternated between thinking that marriage was intrinsically impossible or feeling that I just wasn't cut out for it. Most of the time, I never thought about it at all. But when I met Mallie, it was *easy* to be together. We were instant friends. Companions. And we worked together very well. I was beginning my new career in the personal growth field. Mallie was my constant advisor and confidante. Increasingly, she became my full-time partner. We never even discussed our purpose at first. We didn't have to. We both believed deeply in this new self-help therapy, Rebirthing, and in healing family relationships. There was no question that we were the ones appointed to create a community in New York. It was more like a given than a choice. We were just so good together.

Marriage was the last thing on my mind!

So we were friends who worked together, and who felt this calling to be together and to call people to come together around us. We were both recovering from marriages, however, and were wary of another major commitment. We told each other all the reasons we didn't want to have a relationship. It didn't do any good. We just enjoyed each other so much we kept on choosing to be together. As lovers we blended in such perfect passion that it was as if we had never made love before. It was as if every part of our beings woke up in each other's presence. There were nights we had worked so hard we could hardly love our bodies. We would lie still on our backs and breathe together. Suddenly, the desire to make love would rise out of nowhere, and the heat of passion would drive us together. Being sexual partners seemed not only part of our purpose but a living example of everything we were teaching—breathing, surrender, experiencing oneness, connecting with joy and aliveness. Our love was sweet.

Marriage was the last thing on my mind.

"A difference marriage would make is . . . we'd stop being ourselves and start being who we are not."
"Thank you!"

With Mallie I learned the secrets of love. I learned how to be myself and be in a relationship at the same time. I learned to stay in present time instead of ruining a good time with past projections. I learned how to breathe before responding, that peace needs no defense, that I'd rather win love than arguments. I learned how to enjoy prosperity by providing for a family and sharing with those I love. Instead of conforming to the material world at the expense of the spiritual world or rebelling from the material world in order to be a free spirit, I learned how to build the bridge from the real to the sublime, how to see and feel the extraordinary in the ordinary.

With Mallie, I enjoyed giving so much that I didn't even worry about receiving. I stopped keeping score of how much I got for what I gave and measuring my emotional balance by the difference. We were having too much fun to keep score. We touched each other too deeply to wonder who was doing the touching and who was getting touched. At the point of contact it all felt the same anyway. And being two consenting adults, instead of children, it was a double turn-on for both of us. For the first time in my life I remember thinking, *Lucky me!*

Marriage was the last thing on my mind.

We went to Jamaica and the Virgin Islands, Cape Cod and Bar Harbor, Hollywood, Aspen, Snowmass, Sun Valley, British Columbia and the Yucatan. Sometimes we took the children. Sometimes we went alone. We were on a wonderful honeymoon, and we weren't even married. Why should we think of marriage?

We had our problems, but they were few and far between, and frequently we could resolve them ourselves, and without much fanfare. When we were totally stuck, we'd call in other experts on relationships to advise us.

When a problem arose, we usually held it in the context of our desire to be together forever. Our attitude has always been: *well, this is interesting, but let's get through it fast so we can get back to the good stuff.* Sometimes we had dramatic scenes. I remember one in particular. We were driving through Big Sur with the children. Mallie and I, in the heat of battle, got out of the car and walked over to the edge of a cliff where we went at each other. I remember thinking, what a lovely place to fight. Then I looked back at the car, and I could see the girls' faces pressed against the window. I felt like Mallie and I were inside a television, acting out a soap opera. It was hard to stay serious, but we tried.

We continued to create bizarre games to solve our problems. When we needed to improve our communication, we invented ''The Wet Truth Game.'' We'd get in the tub every night and each communicate withholds from the day, both positive and negative. The only response allowed was ''Thank you!'' So each of us took 100% responsibility for letting go of anything in the way of loving each other unconditionally.

We noticed each of us claimed one side of the bed as a kind of separate territory, and this somehow symbolized what remained of the separation between us. We decided to switch sides of the bed for a while. It was great. Mallie would have my dreams, I'd have hers. When we made love, the balance of female and male energies within and between us was finer. It was such a little game, but the results were great.

Still, marriage was the last thing on my mind!

I learned much from Mallie. She was so grounded in the best of home and family that it was an education to live with her. I could see her unconditional love for the children and me. She was strong in her will and her standards were high, but she was forgiving, not disapproving, and always supportive, though rarely at her own expense. I had never met a woman like her. She held a home, two children, a dog, a cat, and a business together. When she needed to be alone, she'd walk the dog. When she needed a dose of roots, she'd drive up to Vermont and come back with a gallon of pure maple syrup, Vermont cheddar, fresh corn, green peppers, cucumbers, and zucchini. She was the best of country and city all rolled up into one ball of endless energy.

"A difference marriage would make is . . . we'd have to be together 'til death do us part!"

"Thank you!"

One of the greatest gifts Mallie gave me was that she allowed me to face death, not deny it, and in so doing choose life more fully. When my father died, I was driving through a hurricane in Mexico. I came home to Pennsylvania the day of his funeral. I cried. I got angry, but I never quite got the reality of the moment.

I watched Mallie watch her two grandmothers die. She was very close to them. Her pain was almost unbearable—for me. I watched myself want to run away. These were two great Vermont ladies, well into their nineties. As they died, Mallie's heart went out to them; then she pulled herself back together, somehow strengthened by the process. It was very powerful. And miraculous.

What Mallie did made my life easier. What I did made Mallie's life easier. And we both were doing what each of us wanted. For the first time in my life I was experiencing the joy and the freedom of being so aligned with another human being. Here was a woman with whom I could go to a play or a basketball game, watch TV or go to the Cloisters, play cards, discuss politics, literature or metaphysics. Here was my best friend, best lover, best roommate and best business partner! I was happy. I had it all!

Marriage was the last thing on my mind!

It was at a meeting of Certified Rebirthers in 1980. The subject came up. It took us by surprise. We had these meetings three times a year for the purpose of organizing our work, getting clear on new ideas, and clearing our relationships with each other. One of our colleagues popped the question, "What do you two have going on about marriage?" We were too quick to respond. "Marriage?" I said, in a state of shock, "We don't have anything going on about marriage." And Mallie said, "Nothing, nothing at all."

Hearing the tone of our response, we knew we had a lot going on. So we decided to do this process every day. We'd each get three minutes.

"A difference marriage would make is . . . it would lead to divorce."
"Thank you!"

For three months we did this process religiously. It was our intention to keep doing it until nothing came up, then choose whether we really wanted to be married. Secretly, I think we were hoping we'd never complete this process so we'd never have to choose. But, sure enough, it happened. We were in Washington, D.C., about to lead the Loving Relationships Training. We did this process. It kept coming up . . . nothing . . . nothing . . . it wouldn't make any difference.

We were terrified. Being people who fear forward, however, not backward, we chose to be married. But first we called everyone to tell them. We agreed that if there was great resistance among our families, we'd reconsider. We called Mallie's parents, and they thought it was a great idea. We called the kids, and they heartily approved. We called my mom, and she thought it was great. Mallie called her ex-husband, and he said great. I called Kathy, and she said great.

I remember saying to Kathy, "I'm afraid. It's my third chance. Three strikes and you're out."

She responded, "Don't forget, three is a charm!"

We got our marriage license that day. We were married the following Monday. This was neither a Bar Mitzvah nor a neo-Indian ritual. We were married by a friend in a seafood restaurant.

The clams were excellent!

Marriage did make a difference. Much to our surprise, we felt a rush of innocence flood our hearts. As enlightened as we were, I guess there was still a part of us that thought we were living in sin. Getting married, we were as children again, not children trying to walk in their parents' shoes, but children of God blessed in our choice to be one.

Don't get married until you've married yourself!

Once you've discovered your own commitment to yourself, your willingness to be with yourself forever, through good times and bad, then, and only then, do you have the foundation to share the commitment with another. Unconditional love of yourself creates the space in which to experience spiritual union with another.

Marriage can be a trap if you think it is a guarantee of the future. If you expect marriage to provide an external security that will somehow act as a substitute for internal strength, you're in for a surprise and not a wonderful one. There is no ticket you buy at the wedding booth which says, "Destination, Happily Ever After"! The future is what you make it!

Marriage works well when it is an acknowledgment of what is so. Never get married until you "feel" married already! Once you have attained that trust, union, ease, pleasure, and devotion, then you can declare it publicly at a wedding. A marriage ideally is a declaration that another holy relationship has emerged in the world.

You don't want to marry to conform to your parents' ways or to rebel from them. Your marriage should be the perfect expression of your own perfection. You don't want to sacrifice yourself to the institution, or destroy the institution to save your own skin. You want to be in a space where you can function freely in a viable structure, where your internal strength, intuition, and creative energy can blossom, not die, within a system of love. You want your marriage to be an expression of your ability to experience the sublime in the mundane, so that whether you are doing the wash, dishes, or shopping, you can experience your immortal union and purpose together.

Marriage can be the sign that you can experience the extraordinary in the ordinary and no longer have to escape from the reality of life in order to find perfect love!

PUT YOUR MONEY WHERE YOUR HEART IS

"Do you have a couple of singles?"
"Yes. Why?"

In September, 1976, I arrived at JFK with $30 in my pocket. I took a taxi into the city. The meter read $18. "Keep the change!" I told the cabbie as I handed him three tens.

Was I the last of the big time spenders or just plain crazy? Neither. I knew, somewhere in my heart, that whenever I was afraid of running out, it was time for another leap of faith. I had developed a basic trust that the universe would always provide for me. I had learned that whatever I gave would be given back to me, multiplied by the extent that I was willing to receive.

Not that I grew up amid tremendous wealth. On the contrary, Mom and Dad struggled hard to make ends meet. Dad was a lawyer who dabbled in real estate, but he was in love with the underdog, and his love caused him to stay in that role rather than become top dog.

I remember when he owned a tenement on the lower east side. It was during the time when everyone was in an uproar about slumlords. Dad was no slumlord. He would even borrow money to fix his building, putting his tenants' needs above his own. But this did not stop his tenants from calling at all hours of the night to complain about the various emergencies, such as running faucets, leaky toilets, and no heat. He kept waiting for the city to condemn his building, so he could recoup his losses and maybe come out a little ahead. It never happened. It was the end of the Great Society at the time. The government's well of generosity had dried up. The people's desire to help the poor was over. The sixties were giving way to the seventies. The Republicans were taking over.

Mom was frustrated and furious. Their whole life together Dad had told her not to worry, they would retire wealthy and travel around the world. He kept his finances secret, but when he died, she discovered the extent of his debts, and her bitterness almost outweighed her grief. She, and we, had expected wealth.

I remember Dad at the kitchen table the first Sunday of each month. He'd have gotten up at the crack of dawn, gone down to Eldridge Street to collect the rent, and by the time he came home we'd all just be getting up. Most of the money he collected was in cash, and I remember helping him count it. We'd have stacks of hundreds, fifties, twenties, and tens. I thought Dad owned a bank. I must have been 12 at the time.

The contradiction between this image of abundance and Dad dying broke (and broken) tore me apart for many years. But I always knew I would get it together. Indeed, I remember Mom and Dad both telling me I would have it easier. They struggled so I wouldn't have to. They sacrificed so I could relax. It almost seemed my debt to them was to have an easy life, a good life, a rich life.

Unfortunately, I was a rebel like my Dad. And my family financial tradition caused me not to want to play the money game at all. Money seemed like a source of pain, conflict, and disappointment in my family. As a teenager, I avoided any practical advice like the plague.

"What are you going to be?" my mom would ask.

"A millionaire," I would reply, defensively.

"Oh? Do you have a plan?"

"It's none of your business!"

It always seemed like a choice between happiness and money. The only trouble was that I wanted both. I made a secret pact with myself to be a millionaire by the time I was 30 or kill myself. The day before my thirtieth birthday I changed my mind.

In truth, I had no plan. In spirit, I was a rebel like my father, rooting for the underdog, wanting to overthrow a system that would neither house the poor nor feed the hungry. I can now see that during those years I was defending my father's failure by attacking the system that I thought had held him back. Nonetheless, I was learning valuable lessons about money despite myself.

The first thing anyone has to learn about money, and I was no exception, is how to take care of oneself. I had been educated with a lot of false beliefs about money. For one thing, I had been led to believe that the more education one received, the more doors would open and the fatter one's bank account would be. So when I walked out of graduate school at age 26, I was somewhat disconcerted to learn that I didn't automatically have a hotel on Boardwalk and two on Park Place as a natural result of all those big bucks my parents had invested in my "higher" education.

Then, when I thought about it, I realized that if education were the source of wealth, then all the college professors I had studied under would have been millionaires—which was not the case. Except for one. Professor K, taught me logic for four months until one fine spring morning he paused in mid-sentence, puffing his pipe and peering out the window. The pause was quite pregnant and interminably so. Finally, he said, "Excuse me, it's too fine a day to be logical." After which he exited, much to our confusion, never to be seen again. Rumor had it he quit teaching that day and could be found on his yacht in the Caribbean.

Mostly, though, teachers didn't have yachts, which, quite frankly, contributed to my premature departure from the halls of academia.

"Do you have a couple of singles?"
"Yes. Why?"

Another myth about money I learned to let go was that the path to wealth involved gaining a lot of experience at one job, working up the ladder of success. I could see this was blatantly false. If it were true, then civil service workers would end up rich. Indeed, you could start at the bottom and work your way up to President. The American Dream can be very naive, and if you're unconscious, you don't wake up.

Maybe I overreacted to this realization because I refused to accumulate experience at any one job. Over the years I worked at schools, hospitals, banks, restaurants, offices, door-to-door, telephone sales, and theaters. I may have been running away from commitment, but at the same time, I was learning that I could create money, enough to survive at least, at any number of things. I was beginning to see that I was the source of wealth in my life, not the job. I realized that rich people shared only one thing in common, and that was an attitude towards money, a prosperity consciousness which enables them to function easily and pleasurably in the physical universe.

The more I saw that money came from within, the more I rebelled from external structure of any form. When I became a hippie, I struggled in the physical universe because my whole attitude was that rich people are evil, corrupt, power-hungry, greedy, and unhappy. Who would want to be one of them? At the same time, however, I was inadvertently learning another valuable lesson: that you don't need money to survive.

If you stop and think about it, money is a rather recent historical phenomenon. Certainly, people survived prior to any money system whatsoever. They hunted, fished, farmed, and traded to supply their needs. Money was invented simply to make the exchange of goods less cumbersome—it's easier to exchange coins and paper than it is to carry sacks of potatoes to barter for a cow, for instance.

The years I had no money served me well, because I had to learn to rely on the generosity of others, the abundance of the land, and my own creative energy in order to survive. It's true that I accumulated considerable debts during this period, but I also came to see that a debt is just the measure of how much someone trusts you. My debt was just my credit rating in disguise.

When I gave that cabbie my last three ten dollar bills, I was 32 years old, and broke. What was worse was that, despite all the valuable lessons I was learning, I was no closer to having a clear plan than I had been at my Bar Mitzvah, when I made $1,000 for becoming a man. Ah, if I could only become a man every day. But there was no such job vacancy, even in the *New York Times*.

So I got a job at Brew Burger, waiting tables. I was directing a play evenings. My life seemed as divided as ever, Spirit pointing me in one direction and practical needs reminding me of another. True, I had learned a few things about money. Like you don't get rich waiting on tables!

"Do you have a couple of singles?"
"Yes. Why?"

At first I felt discouraged, stuck in the typical New York trap of working in a restaurant by day and a theater by night. But, I knew, in my heart, that I'd do a whole lot better at the tables if I enjoyed it, not resented it. I remembered some of the angry waitresses I had had in my life, frustrated actresses rehearsing Lady Macbeth for my benefit, bitter old maids taking their resentment towards men out on me, ones that served with a scowl, or shoved a dish in front of me as though it were punishment, not nourishment. But give me a server who loves to serve, or at least respects people, and my natural inclination towards human kindness would surface and gladly prosper the palm of her hand.

So, I learned how to serve with a smile on my face, if not a song in my heart. It worked. My tips were almost always considerably larger than those of the other waiters. I would approach the restaurant as if it were a stage set. My part was to enjoy myself, be myself, and have fun with the customers. My last day at Brew Burger, I worked a business luncheon and received a $100 bill as a tip. It was at that moment I knew it was time to move on.

When Mallie and I began working in the self-improvement business, I had the opportunity to relearn this same lesson, namely that one of the secrets of success is to do what you love and love what you do. After all, most people who become wealthy enjoy their work so much that it is often difficult to pull them away from it. When Mallie and I started leading seminars together, we would send a newsletter out every month, with a calendar of events we were presenting. Obviously, for the calendar to be effective, people had to receive it some time before the events scheduled. Each month I would find myself procrastinating about getting the newsletter done.

Why was I doing this? I hated taking the copy down to the printer because the printer was in the middle of the garment center, and that area of the city was particularly repulsive to me. So I would delay the newsletter, getting it out a week or two late, and by the time people received it half the events on the calendar had already happened. Obviously, this did not help to increase our enrollments.

Then, one month, when I delivered the copy downtown, I noticed that an ice cream store had opened next door to the printer. This changed my outlook completely. From then on I would think about going for ice cream instead of going to the printer. I began to complete the newsletter faster, get it downtown faster, and mail it out faster. Lo and behold, our seminars began to increase in size, the money began to roll in, and success became unavoidable. What a difference a chocolate chocolate-chip cone makes!

I learned always to put pleasure before work. I saw that I had been an unwitting victim of the typical work/play division that defines the American work ethic. Briefly stated, most people live their lives according to the following gospel: work now, play later. So you struggle all day so you can play at night or on weekends or for two or three weeks' vacation each year. Except by the time play comes around, you're too exhausted to do anything except recuperate from the struggle. If you look at most people's schedules, they arc filled with responsibilities, struggles, obligations, and necessities. Rarely do you find a person who schedules pleasure first, work second. And if you ask someone why they

are living their lives this way, they will tell you they can't afford to do
it the other way. Yet if you don't develop the habits of prosperity before
you are wealthy, you will either never gain the money you need to relax
or, if you do, you'll still be acting out a basic "struggle pattern" which
will prevent you from enjoying your life.

Life itself is a miracle. And it is love of life that generates a passion for all that life has to offer. When in your heart you are happy just
to be alive, then you can go out into the world and share that happiness,
whether you're at work or at play. It doesn't make a difference! To struggle
for the things outside yourself that you think will bring you happiness
is to put the cart before the horse. It's love of life that makes you happy,
and that's the lesson of the heart, not the wallet.

"Do you have a couple of singles?"
"Yes. Why?"

When I met Mallie, one of the things that impressed me about
her was that she was clearly a woman who could take care of herself.
Unlike my previous relationships, where my women would tend to be
helpless and want me to be their fathers and take care of them (which
I resented because my father, in the end, hadn't really taken care of my
mother), Mallie was a woman grounded in self-sufficiency, rooted in the
earth like a Vermont maple. Not only was she self-sufficient, she was
able to provide for her two daughters at a time when her ex-husband
was hard pressed to lend support. I observed the way Mallie handled
money and saw that she could let it in easily and let it go freely. She
was not stuck in possessing; when it came to cash flow, she was clearly
riding the river of life.

When I moved in with Mallie and the children, each of us knew
we could take care of ourselves. And Mallie was doing okay taking care
of the kids. At first, I was not willing to share the expense of having
a family package with Mallie. Indeed, I was not willing to provide for
Mallie, let alone the children. So we made our first money agreement
in the spirit of peaceful coexistence. I would pay 25% of everything.
Mallie would pay 75% of everything. At the time, this seemed like a
win/win proposition, since Mallie was saving 25% of her bills and I was
receiving food and lodging at a fraction of what it would have cost me
alone. Financially, our arrangement felt fair to both of us.

Emotionally, it was another story. I felt guilty because in my heart I wanted to give more. I had set myself up almost as a third child in Mallie's household. I was receiving so much and giving so little. I could feel everything my parents had given to me and how much I wanted to give back. At the same time, I was still resenting my father for not being there fully, and so I was not willing to be there 100% for Mallie and the children.

I kept trying to justify my feelings. "They're not my children anyway!" I'd say to myself. But it wouldn't feel right. I knew that even if they had been my biological children, I would have had the same feelings. "They didn't come from my womb!" I would have been thinking. I guess I was feeling the basic resentment most parents go through about having to provide for helpless children. Maybe it's just our own feelings of helplessness we resent. Maybe that's why we don't want to take care of the poor. They remind us too much of the "poor me" part of each of us. We'd just as soon sweep our helplessness under the rug and pretend we don't care.

Only we do. I knew God had sent me this family package, which I still tended to view as more of a time bomb than a gift from heaven. I knew I would never be happy as a man unless I surrendered to giving my all to a woman and her children. I even knew if I agreed to be the provider, God would be more of a provider for me. I knew that it would all come back multiplied, if I would only let go!

While I was going through all of this, Mallie was going through her part. She had grown up the only girl of five children in a family that literally lived from hand to mouth. One of Mallie's early money memories is of her father's reticence about signing a loan that would allow her to go to college. Although he relented, the family tradition was one of living within considerable limits, according to one's means, as they say. In her first marriage, her husband tried several enterprises, including starting a newspaper in their home, and he amassed substantial debts by the time they were divorced. His real love was sailing, with which Mallie was not thrilled, and she chose to go to work to provide the stability he lacked. By the time I met her, I think her main thoughts about money were, "I can do it by myself!" and "Why won't you help?" Mallie's birth was a forceps delivery, and she has always had this ambivalence between thinking she can do it all by herself but wanting more support from others. (If you are a forceps delivery, you tend to have the thought that support is painful.)

"Do you have a couple of singles?"
"Yes. Why?"

After a month of my paying 25% of the expenses, Mallie and I renegotiated our basic money agreement. We had both learned that the purpose of agreements is to serve both parties. We also knew that since agreements should serve us, we shouldn't be slaves to them, and that we always had the right to renegotiate. So we made our agreements for a month at a time, experimenting with what seemed to work and, at the same time, served our growth the most.

I agreed to up my share to 50%. That felt much better to me for a while. Fifty/fifty, what could be fairer? Isn't that what a good relationship is founded on? You take responsibility for your own share; I'll do the same for my half. So there we were, with our separate but equal bank accounts in a separate but equal relationship. It felt much better up to a point.

As the month went on, I began to notice that I was not at all satisfied with this "separate but equal" stuff. What I really wanted in my heart of hearts was not "separate but equal" at all, but rather union with diversity. I wanted that oneness with Mallie which I felt with myself. I wanted to extend that sense of spiritual union I had found with God, myself, and the universe into a primary loving relationship. I wanted to give my all and have it all. I wanted to be 100% responsible, not fifty. And I wanted Mallie to be 100% there for me, not fifty. The more I thought about it, the more I could see that the way we chose to handle money in our relationship was the exact same way we were choosing to handle the relationship itself.

If two people each take 100% responsibility for the whole, then you have two creators, two whole beings sharing the whole of the relationship. This fifty/fifty stuff was really a Mexican stand-off. It was saying, we are two separate human beings and the closest we can ever come to being one is to meet at the border of our separation. This statement was inconsistent with our spiritual beliefs. We were out of integrity in being separate but equal financially while claiming we were one spiritually. No wonder the second month was uneasy for me.

And so the third month Mallie agreed to support me and the children alone. This was a big step for both of us. It enabled me to surrender beyond my guilt to my total appreciation of being provided for, by my parents, by God, by my friends, strangers and, indeed, the entire universe. For Mallie, it represented a leap past her resentment into a new level of abundance, gratitude, and success. As I let go of my guilt, and Mallie let go of her resentment, it was inevitable that our prosperity would increase. And it did.

The fourth month I chose to provide for all four of us. This was another enormous leap. I was expressing my commitment to the whole family to take care of them, to be there for them, to make sure they always had enough. Mallie was surrendering to her willingness to trust a man to back her up as no man had done in her life. It was during this month that I urged Mallie to quit her job and work with me full time. I was inspired by my own willingness to be a provider. I wanted in my heart to be a real man, and for me a real man was one who was willing to accept dominion over family. I somehow felt I was making God happy, and that even my dad in heaven was smiling at my success, though his had been incomplete.

As month five began, we seemed to have stretched our prosperity consciousness to its max. There was only one problem remaining: we still had separate accounts. Pooling all our monies in joint banking accounts was an emotional merger for both of us. For one thing, I had a surprising number of accounts spread out across the country, and it took a while even to find all the passbooks, let alone write to the banks, close old accounts, sign new signature cards, and so on. At times, I would even forget an account—trying to hide yet another thing from myself and Mallie.

In the old days I would only have one savings account, but I had learned that this didn't support my prosperity consciousness. To have only one account is to save for a rainy day. The only way you get to use your savings is to create some emergency in your life which justifies making a withdrawal. One of the advantages of having multiple savings accounts is that it generates more money. It's like saying to the universe: *Okay, I'm going to give you lots of space to give to me. I am open in many ways to receiving. Shower me with money!*

Mallie and I opened a "Travel Account" at the Cape Cod Savings Bank, because the Cape symbolized our desire to travel at that time. In New York, we opened a "Cash Flow Account," a "Financial Independence Account," a "Large Purchase Account," and an "Investment Account." Mind you, we opened these accounts with small deposits in each. But our excitement about saving for all these different purposes motivated us to earn more money and to distribute it quickly to all our stashes. It is fun to watch money grow!

> *"Do you have a couple of singles?"*
> *"Yes. Why?"*

Two self-sufficient people, when they join forces in a relationship, should generate tremendous wealth. Mallie and I learned, through our changing monthly money agreements, that each of us was capable of supporting the entire family. This gave us great certainty, as well as security. Psychologically, I knew that both Mallie and I were supporting me, and Mallie knew that both of us were supporting her. It almost felt, therefore, that there were four of us, not two, working for our relationship. How could our money not grow? Together we were more than the sum of our separate earning powers.

On the other hand, if two people come into a relationship without certainty of their individual self-sufficiency, they can experience a financial strain and drain by virtue of being together. In such cases, I recommend keeping the money separate for a while, until such time as both parties know they can make it on their own.

Even after we formed one money pool, I experienced reluctance and resistance about how much I was called upon to give. I remember one Christmas when Mallie and I were spending a small fortune on gifts for the children. The more money we spent, the angrier I got. Being a Jew, I think I had a basic negative attitude towards Christmas to begin with. As a child, I always felt excluded from the abundance that was Christmas for my friends. My birthday is December 11th, and it always seemed as though Jesus was upstaging my birth. Well, this particular Christmas I was spending more on the children than anyone had ever spent on me. Part of me wanted to be the receiving child rather than the giving parent. Christmas Eve I was steaming. I stormed out of our apartment and went for a late-night walk. My pockets were loaded with several $100 bills. As I walked down the street, my blood boiling with resentment, I felt footsteps behind me. Then I felt a gun in my back.

"Give me all your money!" a young voice said.

I thought about Mallie, the kids, Christmas, my selfishness, and I started to laugh uncontrollably.

"Your money!" the voice repeated.

I reached into my pocket, considering giving only a part of what

I had. But I felt that God wanted me to give all. This was clearly a lesson in surrendering and letting go. I wasn't even frightened by the gun. I gave thought to running away, or spinning around and slugging the kid. But I chose to hand over all five $100 bills and say " Merry Christmas!" The kid, totally surprised by how much money I had, and confused by my generous attitude, said, "Thank you," and ran off. I was laughing hard as I returned home to play Santa Claus and put the gifts under the tree. It was amazing how much was there. I felt totally grateful that I had so much to give. And I had learned that I could always afford to be generous.

"Do you have a couple of singles?"
"Yes. Why?"

Speaking of resentment, I might as well mention my relationship with the IRS. I had never been self-employed before, and I was not accustomed to having to deal with taxes. When your taxes are withheld, it's far easier to give to Uncle Sam than when you have to do it yourself. All my rebellion resurfaced at the thought of paying the government for defense, nuclear development, and the like. I just couldn't do it. A friend advised us to open a special "Tax Account" for this purpose, but we procrastinated for weeks, months, years. Mallie had a dislike for taxes, too, probably because her dad had overpaid the government rather than get the refunds due him. I'm sure she felt somewhere that the government owed her money.

As our income was rapidly increasing, our unpaid taxes were accumulating with equal speed. We felt guilty, out of integrity, and stuck, but for years we couldn't bring ourselves to handle this area of our life. We wanted to be a legitimate business, we were feeling more gratitude than ever, but when it came to Uncle Sam we held back. In the back of my mind was the thought that the only certainties in life were death and taxes, so if I didn't pay my taxes I would live longer. This was not conscious, not premeditated, but looking back at the intensity of my feelings around this issue I have to admit I felt a life and death urgency at the time. Still, we didn't pay.

It was a torrid summer day when lightning struck! I was playing basketball in a schoolyard when suddenly I felt my ankle crack and I went down in agony. I had severely sprained my ankle, which forced me to be flat on my back for several weeks. (I could walk with crutches, but preferred not to.) As soon as my ankle turned, I thought, *Taxes!*

There was no way I could avoid such a clear message. It was time for me to get my house completely in order. My accountant advised me to go through all my files, reconstructing my income and expenses (and, indeed, my life) for the last five years. It was quite an experience! I lay in my bed, remembering my life as it had unfolded over that period of time. I cried at images I had tried to suppress. I grew angry at events where I had sold out. I breathed heavily, moving all these past incompletions through, and out, of my body. When the three weeks had passed, I was ready to face Uncle Sam, if not God Himself.

Restoring integrity to my tax situation went a long way to healing what was left of my resentment to my father. The IRS is a super-father figure for most people, and the feelings we have about Big Brother watching over us are intimately connected to how we felt as children when our parents disapproved of us. To forgive my father was to forgive all fathers and father figures, even politicians I didn't agree with and presidents I didn't choose. I realized how grateful I was for being an American and that, no matter how opposed I was to specific policy decisions, my love for my motherland was firm and proud. There is no other country on this earth I would rather have as my home.

> *"Do you have a couple of singles?"*
> *"Yes. Why?"*

Becoming homeowners was a big move for Mallie and me. We had lived in much too small an apartment for a couple of years, when one day a co-op plan dropped in our laps. The offer was so good that we could not afford to turn it down. We had no problem raising the money. Everything was going oh-so-easy. We felt as though God had given us some wonderful gift for our efforts in His behalf. Lucky us!

Unfortunately, neither of our families had ever owned a home, so we had no family tradition to continue in this area. One thing I've learned, whenever you are about to surpass your family in some significant way, you must always release something—another link to your familiar past must be broken. Both Mallie's father and my own (although he owned that tenement) had avoided opportunities to buy homes for their families. I always used to pressure my dad to buy a house outside the city where we could live in more peace and quiet. Dad was a street kid at heart, though, and his love of the neighborhood in Brooklyn was a mighty thing. It took me a long time to forgive Dad for keeping us stuck in the city. As soon as I was old enough, I had abandoned New York, hit the road, and lived in fifteen different homes in the ten years I was gone. When I returned to the Big Apple to reconnect with my roots, I was still too disconnected from myself to have my own home. So it was perfect that Mallie had a home I could move into.

When the day came to complete the purchase of our co-op, I could feel a silent tension building between Mallie and me. I don't think we took a breath between us that whole day. We went downtown to an office building, where all the legal procedures went ever so smoothly. We walked out in a daze, went out to a Japanese restaurant to celebrate. Almost immediately I felt the urge to fight.

"When are we going to sell it?" I said.

"What?" Mallie was astonished.

"I think we should sell it quick and get out of the city."

"We just bought it."

"So what?"

"Can't we celebrate before we discuss selling it?"

I was furious. I didn't even know why. There was no logic to my feelings. Looking back, I know I was feeling all the anger I had ever suppressed for never having had the home I wanted. Also, I was feeling guilty for having more than my family had had. I guess the past just came exploding out of me. In any case, I ruined the *sake* with my fury, and the sushi with my rage.

"Do you have a couple of singles?"
"Yes. Why?"

One night I was watching TV in bed when I noticed Mallie doing something that blew me away. She had cut out hundreds of discount coupons from newspapers and magazines and was sorting her piles on the bed. I suddenly flashed back to a similar scene, twenty years earlier, when I saw my mother doing the exact same thing. At the time I got angry with my mother, asking her why she had to worry about nickels and dimes. I didn't like to be reminded of our financial limitations as a child and wanted to keep the image of my father's stacks of cash in mind, not my mother's stacks of coupons. Watching Mallie, I forgave my mother. I saw that frugality and prosperity were not opposed to each other, but were really two sides of the same coin. I saw Mallie, with her poor Vermont background, and my mom, with her Depression conscious-ness, as teaching me a valuable lesson in how to save money.

Along these same lines, both Mallie and my mother love to enter contests. I had never given much thought to such money games, sweepstakes, and lotteries Mallie was entering. In my mind, you never won contests, and certainly couldn't count on winning something for nothing as a way of life. Mallie kept on entering. She made an agree-ment not to enter any contest that would cost more than a postage stamp to enter. She received contest newsletters and read the prizes to me at night. I began to think, well, maybe . . .

Mallie was also processing her thoughts on winning and losing, wanting to develop a winning attitude that would result in big wins. She read articles about people who won, who had somehow beat the system, or shall I say, harnessed the system for their benefit. I began to get into it more and more. I realized I had the thought *I never win anything*, and that this thought alone could hold Mallie back by association. I knew that my thoughts were creative—that I was the thinker—and I used my spiritual enlightenment, as did Mallie, to turn a losing attitude into a winning one. Mallie kept on entering.

One day the phone rang. Mallie had won a one week vacation to Bermuda for two, all expenses paid, plus a substantial cash bonus. We couldn't believe it. It was too good to be true. But to demonstrate just how much resistance we had to receiving something for nothing, it took us almost a full year to use this prize. We kept putting off going to Bermuda. It was as if we had to work for another year to justify tak-ing the gift. And when we did go to Bermuda, what we discovered is that, much as we enjoyed the holiday, a week of financial independence was as much as we could tolerate. It was very threatening to our work ethic to bathe in the generosity of the universe. *Now* I'd like to win a million dollars and confront my work ethic a little more!

"Do you have a couple of singles?"
"Yes. Why?"

While I was learning about money, one of my teachers suggested I carry a $100 bill in my wallet at all times. The rule was, I could never spend this hundred unless I could replace it with another hundred the next day. I loved this process. I would walk down the street, window shop-ping, and where I might have thought: *I can't afford that,* now I said: *Well,*

I could buy it, but do I really want it?

I loved $100 bills so much I began to gather more and more of them. Once I even had Mallie give me a money massage, gently rubbing me with all my hundreds so that I could get the idea that money was a pleasurable thing, not a painful burden.

Often I would have ten $100 bills in my wallet, and nothing else. I could make large purchases, but when it came to small items, I would always ask Mallie for a few extra dollars here and there. This was a relatively small lesson, but I realized that I was still setting up Mallie to be my mother, and, in a sense, pay for my immediate needs and give me an allowance. We'd be riding along in a taxi, for example, and when we'd get to our destination, the cabbie would say, "Four dollars!" I'd open my wallet, count my hundreds, see nothing else, and ask Mallie,

> *"Do you have a couple of singles?"*
> *"Yes. Why?"*

Put your money where your heart is! If you love someone 100%, support them 100%—emotionally, spiritually, and financially. Two individuals who have mastered the relationship between love and money are a business team to be reckoned with.

Every year's end, on New Year's Eve, Mallie and I sit down and write our gratitudes for the previous year and our goals for the coming one. It is totally empowering to align our minds as well as our hearts. The union of love and money is the second marriage of heaven and earth, which I believe is God's intention for all His children.

Money is energy in motion! Money is a medium of exchange! The way you handle money in a relationship is usually a perfect mirror of the way you handle the relationship itself. Do you hold back in giving money to your partner? Are you generous? Do you trust the give and take? Do you keep score on how much you give and how much you receive and is your emotional balance a function of the difference?

Love and money tend to be separate in our minds, and we need to marry the two in our hearts. After all, the language of love and the language of money have many common terms. "How much are you WORTH to yourself?" is a question that can apply to your financial worth or your self-esteem. "How much do you appreciate or value yourself?" is a similar question.

In fact, you are already in possession of something more valuable than all the money in the world. And that is life itself. You would not trade your life for a million dollars, which means you're already a millionaire in self-worth. It's important to stop and acknowledge this, because it is from love of life itself that all other riches spring forth. The more you are grateful for life, the more life gives you to be grateful for.

Clear your mind of all your negative thoughts about money. If you think money corrupts, think about all the corrupt, poor people, and realize that corruption comes from within, not without. If you think that it's better to give than to receive, don't be surprised at your bank statement at the end of the month. Your thoughts about money produce results about money, so make sure your results are consistent with your heart's desires. If not, you are free to change your mind.

In a relationship, things are easiest when both people take responsibility for the whole, not just their halves. This is true financially, as well as emotionally. When each person can support the whole relationship, then you have the basis for becoming wealthy together. There is no good reason on Earth why a successful relationship should not also be reflected materially. The world of spirit and the world of matter need to be bridged, not severed. The material kingdom is not a distraction from spiritual growth; it is the arena in which we can clearly measure our growth.

It is my firm belief that a couple who surrenders to the full expression of their personal union will inevitably experience benefits in all areas of their life. You can really have it all together. So choose to play the love and money game as a team.

CHOSEN CHILDREN

"Let go of my arm!"
"No!"

As I chose to own my home more and more, I also came to "own" the two children I had somehow inherited. At first it was not easy. I didn't want to be their father; they didn't want to be my children. And I certainly was not thrilled at the thought of being a stepfather. The very mention of the word still sends chills up and down my spine. Besides, I was supporting the kids in having a good relationship with their biological father. Wasn't it good enough that I loved their mother and provided for them financially?

Still, by virture of my role as the only adult male of the house, I began to assume more and more of a fatherly pose. I remember reacting unconsciously to the children's demands at first. I would see myself doing and hear myself saying the things my parents had done and said to me—things I had sworn I would never do or say. (Never say never—it is usually a clear indication that you are resisting something you need to heal. And what you resist usually persists!)

I remember one time the girls were fighting, as they tended to do, and I couldn't stand it. I guess it reminded me of all the fighting in my own family. "Go to your room!" I screamed at the top of my lungs, scaring the kids almost as much as I scared myself. My body was shaking from the intensity of my feeling. I could really feel how we take out the resentment towards our own parents on our children, especially when they act in the same ways our own parents disapproved. Whenever I hollered at the children, I actually felt *hollered at*, more than *angry at* them.

In each of us there is a parent and a child. The inner child is often crying out for the unconditional love, acceptance, holding and nurturing it never got enough of as a child. Part of growing up to be a healthy adult (as opposed to a functioning grown-up) is learning how to give this inner child everything it needs and deserves. Since we tend to act out our incomplete relationship with ourselves with other people, the way we feel around children is often a clear barometer of how we relate to the child within. For me, having Kim and Suzie in my home, and allowing them all the way into my heart, has been a miraculous healing process between the adult me and the child me.

But even as I could see the value of the process I was going through with them, a part of me balked at the thought of being their father. They were not my creation, I thought. Why should I be responsible? I'll never really be their father anyway, so what's the use in pretending?

My mind was very limited at the time. Somewhere in my consciousness I was associating the dream of killing my father, burying him in the closet, and having to live with his clone, with the illegitimacy I felt as a father figure in my adult home. If I couldn't accept my own father as my real father, how the hell could I accept myself as father of children I never had?

Nonetheless, I had to live with them, and so, inevitably I grew into fathering more. I was awkward in the beginning. I was confused between the need for freedom and the need for discipline, an issue I was still working on in my own life. How could I be clear on this for them if I was in conflict myself? I could see how they would act out the suppressed, unresolved feelings I had. The worst was when they fought, and Kim and Suzie had some humdingers. I would always be tempted to take sides, to make one of them right and one of them wrong. But this never worked, because as soon as I took sides, they would join forces, defend each other, and gang up on me. I began to think I was going at it the wrong way. I had to find the place in my heart where I could treat them both equally, not blame either, and love them unconditionally rather than be Big Brother watching.

I have already described how deeply I felt for Kim and Suzie. But loving and having a successful loving relationship are two different items. I didn't know how to love someone and say no to them. I felt so guilty for saying no to the kids that I would shut my heart down, in self defense, and be too aggressive in my demands. This overracting caused me to be seen as a figure to be feared, rather than respected. I felt lost as a father. Sometimes I would think Mallie and I should have another child, just to balance the household a little more. But then I would think, how can I have another child when I am not even capable of handling the ones I have been given?

"Let go of my arm!"
"No!"

I began to make parenting one of my passionate areas of study. I began to think back to the days I taught at a boarding school and how all the kids would flock to my house for solace from the administration. I could see how, although I was part of the staff, Director of Theater Arts to be specific, emotionally I was much more aligned with the rebellious teenagers. I definitely did not want to be a parental figure for the kids, but the more I resisted the powers that be, the more I became a parent, if not a local hero, for many of the children. At the time I thought I was providing a sadly missing service for the kids, a kind of halfway house between home and school. Looking back, I can now see how I was halfway between being a child and a grownup myself.

As Mallie and I began to develop a following, the same family patterns began to emerge. It was amazing how quickly we became mother and father to a large spiritual family of seekers and searchers. Most of them were running away from home in some form or another. We knew quite well that whatever is unresolved with your parents comes up in your other relationships for healing. In fact, this was the theme of the Loving Relationships Training, which we were promoting in the world. And so we encouraged all of our students and clients to make peace with the past, to let go of their need for their parents' approval and/or their desire to get even with them for not giving them what they had wanted as children. We asked anyone who worked with us to write letters of completion to their mom and dad, to take responsibility for what they had created in the past, to forgive themselves and their parents, and to tell the truth about how they felt and why. As our students went through this family healing process, they reported remarkable transformations in all their relationships, with lovers, with friends, co-workers, bosses, and others. Mallie and I felt validated in the direction we were supporting others in taking.

At the same time, I was noticing a pattern developing among some of my more advanced students. They would grow rapidly at first, their self–esteem increasing as they acknowledged their equality to their parents and made friends with the authorities they used to fear and/or resent. Then they would reach a certain point in their process when they would rebel from the very teachings and teachers that taught them to get through this pattern. It was a paradox. The more we said "Forgive your parents" the more they would do so, and then transfer the whole cycle to us. We lost several potential leaders in our community this way, not to mention dear friends.

"Let go of my arm!"
"No!"

When I thought about what was happening, I had to admit that I was still unresolved vis-a-vis my father, and I was creating this drama outside myself so I could be more aware of the split inside me I needed to heal. I realized that I had a very limited view of how one grows, and that my finest students were simply following in my own footsteps. In my life, and in my mind, the way you grew was to find a teacher, learn everything he had to teach, then stand up to him to demonstrate your self-esteem and equality, and reclaim the power you had given away, and then move on. This was how I had grown. I found someone I admired, learned the system they were teaching, then rebelled and moved on. Why should anyone do it any other way since my way had worked so well for me? Was there even another way? And if so, what was it? Was it better? Easier? I had no answers.

So there I was, an acknowledged leader and parental figure, an authority on relationships for many hundreds of people, yet I was still a closet rebel. In the back of my mind I was still rooting for the underdog, secretly supporting their rebellion, even at my own expense. I was clearly caught in a double bind: I wanted to be a parent without rebellious children, yet I believed that the way children grew into adults was by rebelling. What to do, what to do. . . .

At the same time our community in New York was growing, we were travelling more and more all over the world to give seminars, workshops, and trainings. We were spreading the good word about loving relationships. But Kim and Suzie were not happy with our lifestyle at all. Why should they be? We were like the renegade kids who got to run away from home, while they were like the parents who stayed home, often with friends of ours they loved but who were not parents, waiting for us to return. Everything was topsy-turvy at home. Often the children would fight, Kim, being the oldest, trying to be a parent to Suzie, who would then have none of it. I think they were just crying out for attention.

Even when we were home, our apartment was so flooded with our spiritual family that the kids often felt like second class citizens. There would be all these clients of ours, projecting their family needs onto us, and often we would neglect Kim and Suzie just to take care of business. When your business is relationships and you operate out of your home, there is no way to sweep feelings under the carpet.

We would have heated family meetings where we would all try to express our needs and frustrations. Often we'd scream at each other just to be heard. We all loved each other so much. The kids especially would do anything not to make our lives more difficult. They became very independent very quickly. But we paid a price for it. It clearly did not work to be parttime parents. We were teaching the value of being 100% responsible (which is not to say obligated) in all loving relationships, but when it came to the children we were not practicing what we preached.

It seemed like everyone wanted us to be their parents, and all we wanted was to have the freedom from our own, at least in our minds. It's funny how people wait for their parents to give them freedom. Even as adults, we hold ourselves back, psychologically dependent on someone else's permission in order to feel free to do what we want. Yet, when you think about it, freedom is not something that is given or taken away. I know there are countries, cultures, and families where there is less allowed than could be. But freedom itself is a matter of the heart; it is an internal state of being that can only be denied by oneself. You are, in essence, free to think whatever you want, feel however you want, and do as you please. Of course, so is everyone else. Part of what we call freedom is the willingness to accept the consequences of other people's reactions to our doing as we please. Often it seems as though we have only two choices: either to please others at our own expense (conformity) or to please ourselves at others' expense (rebellion). Neither course of action produces satisfaction. What growing up is, to a large extent, is learning a win/win philosophy and how to practice this. It is possible for you to please yourself and others at the same time, without sacrifice or compromise. But in order to experience this truth, you must first entertain the possibility of such a cooperative, not competitive state of relationships.

The more I thought about it, the more I saw that there was really no escape from freedom, nor from the personal responsibility that entailed. But before I could reclaim my own freedom, I had to set my parents free a little more, especially my father. I had somehow to find the way to accept them as they were, not try to change the way it was or had been, to surrender to the perfection of the family I had chosen.

> *"Let go of my arm!"*
> *"No!"*

One thought that kept me stuck was that I hadn't chosen my parents, so why should I be obligated to accept them? It's funny, but it was the same feeling I had about Kim and Suzie. One day a teacher of mine suggested that I had chosen my parents. He proceeded to have me close my eyes, do a deep relaxation, and begin to imagine my own conception.

Now, I don't have the greatest memory. Sometimes I forget what happened yesterday, and often I misplace my keys, wallet, or whatnot. Nor am I certain I believe in reincarnation in theory, let alone in actuality. I was raised to be skeptical and, no matter how spiritual I happened to be feeling, there was always this part of me that questioned everything. I had, however, had some profound memories of my birth while rebirthing, so I would not deny that there were memories lodged in me that I was not connected to. But conception?

I decided to go along with the meditation. I chose not to worry whether it was memory or imagination and that whatever I saw was valid and relevant, at least emotionally. I saw myself as a free, disembodied spirit floating through the universe. I was a flash of light with total awareness. It was time to choose a body and I was searching the universe for the perfect circumstances for this embodiment. The questions kept popping up: Why Earth? Why America? Why Jewish? Why Mom and Dad? And gradually it became clear, all the choices I had made in the first place, my reasons for being here, and how my path had been perfect all along.

I saw that I chose to be born at the right time and place, that part of my purpose was to be an instrument of peace. (I was a war baby and, although my parents wanted a son, they didn't want a soldier.) I chose to be Jewish to complete all my wanderings, find the meaning of family, accept myself as one of the chosen, and implement my vision of the promised land. I chose my mother to show me that the reservoir of love is infinite, and I chose my father to teach me a fiery spirit of independence, as well as a passion for adventure, travel, people, and places. I chose my sister to inspire me to read, write, learn everything I needed to get everything I wanted. I chose to be a man because one of my major lessons in this life is to learn how to be the man of the house. I could not have chosen a better home to learn this lesson.

> *I'm a family man!*
> *I'm a businessman!*
> *I'm a man of the world!*
> *I'm a man of peace!*
> *I have everything I need*
> *to get everything I want;*
> *I want to live in peace!*

In connecting to my original choices for being here, it became much easier to feel all the choices I had made in my life, even the ones that seemed off-purpose. I could see that all of life was based on creative choice, and that my creative energy was unlimited, and the options were infinite. Of course, I had chosen the children Mallie had given me. Indeed, in choosing Mallie I was choosing them, and that was as much a choice as any father had ever made. Sometimes I even thought that the biological idea of conception was a myth. I mean, I could understand the biology of the process, but still, it all seemed like a miracle to me. Science never really explains why things happen, only how. Maybe all conceptions are really immaculate, and sex is God's way of giving us pleasure while He is doing His thing.

I also came to see how I chose my life every day, that each day was a process of re-creation of one's life. Certainly, every day I chose Mallie I was more deeply committed to her. And each day I chose the children I felt more like a father and less like an intruder. I realized that being a parent is a continuous series of choices, not just conception, pregnancy and birth. Look at all the parents who abort their children, or give them up for adoption. What is a real parent if not someone who chooses to parent his creations day by day?

> *"Let go of my arm!"*
> *"No!"*

One of the choices I had made was to be tall. As a child, I was always disturbed by my parents' shortness. I wanted to be six feet tall.

My father totally supported this goal, and would measure my height frequently to see how I was doing. I remember standing against a wall, stretching upwards as much as I could (sometimes I would sneak up on my toes a little, but usually Dad would catch me cheating and push me down a notch) and Dad would scratch a pencil mark in the wall to mark the spot. When I was nine, my father took me to his office one Saturday, as he often did, and a colleague of his remarked that I would never be tall because Dad was five foot six. Both Dad and I grew furious. What did he mean? I could be as tall as I wanted. The choice was mine!

When I was 14, I was rapidly approaching my goal. I remember I was taller than Dad. And I was feeling a lot of strength in my body. The thought occurred to me that I probably could take Dad if it came down to it. My father was not a punitive person. As I mentioned before, I think he had been somewhat abused as a child, and his greatest fear was that he would take his anger out on me. This caused him to be a little removed from me, and it wasn't until recently that I realized this was because he loved me so much he didn't want to hurt me. My mother was in charge of my discipline, although Dad would often complain that she wasn't doing a thorough job.

Dad never hit me. But one day that male energy came up between us. I think I was trying to prove that I could stand up to him, be his equal, even take over for him should anything happen. I know I had a lot of incestuous feelings at the time, and I'm sure I had the desire to replace my father and be a better husband to my mother than he was. I really don't know what was going on that day, but I'm sure Freud would have had a field day. What I do remember is two tempers clashing. Dad and I were blasting each other full force. We were shaking in rage. Dad lifted his arm to smack me, as he had never done before. I reached out and grabbed his arm. I could feel all the strength in my arm, and it was enough to hold Dad off. I'm as strong as my father, I was thinking, and a mixture of glee and terror gripped me.

"Let go of my arm!"
"No!"

I wouldn't let go. It was almost as if I was paralyzed in this grip. It was so exhilarating! Then, suddenly, the strong man in me disappeared, and the helpless child reared his head, and I released my hold and went crying to my room. I felt as though I had violated some sacred code of father-son relationships. That I had shown up my dad as being vulnerable, and that I didn't want to see his weakness. I wanted him always to be stronger than me, so he would take care of me forever, and I could stay a child. My shame was overwhelming. I could feel Dad's pain, probably from when his father had beaten him—it was a load he always carried.

We go through three stages of perception regarding our parents. At first, they seem like almighty beings, perfect in every way, the best of all possible parents, indeed the only parents in our eyes. Then we grow up, look around a little, rebel a little, and gradually our perception changes. We become disillusioned with our parents, see their shortcomings, problems and inconsistencies. We throw them off the pedestal we had so innocently placed them on. For many people, the process stops here, and they remain out of balance in their feeling towards their parents. Those who complete the process, however, must come full circle, and see that the disillusionment is as much of an illusion as the original illusion. They let go of the past, forgive their parents completely and, in so doing, see the perfection of the process they shared in growing up with mom and dad.

My fight with my father was revived in the fights with my own children. I remember one time, Kim and I really had it out. This was early on in our relationship, one of those times I abruptly halted the fight by shouting, "Go to your room!" She, and Suzie, stormed into the room, slamming the door behind them. It was a hot summer night. Kim started screaming at the top of her lungs. The door was stuck from the humidity. She screamed how she was going to call the police, her "real" dad, that I was guilty of child abuse, and so on. All my worst fears of being a father were right there before my eyes and ears. I was ready to call it quits at that moment, but, at the same time, I saw that I was going through some primitive ritual which was empowering me more as a father. Still, I didn't like it.

Another time, several years later, Kim and I went at it again. She was going through her rebellious period, and I was fed up. With Kim and me there was rarely any build-up to a fight. It would be all or nothing. We'd just explode out of nowhere, scream at each other, then end up crying, hugging and apologizing. And our fights, thank God, were few and far between. I remember the last one. Again, I had told her to go to her room, but this time she refused. I grabbed her, intending to carry her to her room, but Kim was always great with her hands.

She could untie knots, knit, tickle me, or scratch me like no one I had ever met. As I felt her nails dig into me, I started wrestling with her, just trying to contain her and literally save my own skin. She raised her arm to strike me. I grabbed it.

"Let go of my arm!"
"No!"

The tables were turned. There I was, in my father's position, and there she was, in mine. The resemblance was unmistakable. I was shaking with the same fear and trembling that had been in my body at 14. I released my grip.

The creative urge is, in a sense, the desire to parent. And parenting is largely about nourishing our creations until they achieve complete independence. Sometimes these creations are projects, like a work of art, a novel or a business project; other times they are actual children. In a sense the act of creation starts with any thought, or concept, that you are willing to follow through from conception to actuality. To parent either a project or a child, is to learn how to give of yourself fully and freely. If you don't give freely, you will be stuck in resentment, sacrifice, and martyrdom, and you will miss the joy of parenting completely.

Often, the most difficult stage of parenting for the parent is the final process of letting go. Especially during the middle teenage years, when a child is half adult and half infant and you are receiving mixed messages about their needs, it can be difficult to choose how much to hold on and how much to let go. But there comes a time when parent and child must let go of each other for growth to continue. The umbilical cord is cut at birth, often too soon, before it has stopped pulsating, before the newborn has had the opportunity to learn how to use its breathing apparatus, before it has let go of the amniotic fluid in its lungs. But the cord is cut physically at birth.

There are psychological, energetic cords between parents and children, however, and indeed between people in relationships of any sort, and these invisible cords are subtle but powerful entanglements in our lives. To let go of the subtle cords between a child and a parent is a gradual process. I'm sure it can be a peaceful process, though in my life violence always threatened the separation to the extent that I thought my umbilical attachment to my parents was what kept me alive. To let go of these cords is to acknowledge that your parents were never the source of your aliveness, and that you are an independent source of life energy, not dependent on an outside generator. To the extent that we believe our parents to be the source of our power, we use them as an outlet for our rage and frustrations. When I released Kim from my grip, I was also releasing my need to conquer my father in order to absorb his power. Conquest is always based on a feeling of not being enough to oneself. So we always need to possess more in order to fill up the void we are afraid of experiencing inside ourselves.

> *"Let go of my arm!"*
> *"No!"*

In the last analysis, I saw that it had been God's arm I was wrestling with all along. The root of all rebellion is rebellion from God, and by God I don't mean any particular religious description but rather Beingness Itself. I realized that I resented God for giving me freedom and the hugeness of that responsibility. You'd have to be a God yourself to handle that level of freedom. Yes, I had to forgive God for giving me freedom, even though I valued it next to life itself as my most precious possession.

Letting go of the rebellion from God, the Father of all creation, empowered me to be more of a creative father in my own life, both in terms of the children I had been given and the projects I was delivering into reality. I could see how I had always projected my dad onto God and God onto my dad, and how, together, they were a fearsome combination in my mind. God, the Father, and my old man were more like Grand Inquisitors than benevolent parents. I would fear their punishments more than look forward to their rewards. In letting go of God's arm, I released my dad's as well. In coming to see that I was a chosen child of God, I chose both God and my father more fully, and these children of mine, Kim and Suzie, who had arrived in my heart so circuitously. I guess God does operate in mysterious ways. But the mystery's half the fun of it. The other half is in the detective work it spawns.

A successful parent is one in touch with his own creative urge! You can parent a child, a project, or, indeed, any thought, but to do it successfully you must take responsibility not only for the conception, but the delivery and release of this concept into the world.

To the extent that we are incomplete with our own parents, who in our minds created us, we are bound to be incomplete with parenting anything. If you have children, they will remind you of the helpless child within you that needs to be held, hugged, reassured. If you are still stuck in resenting your parents for what they didn't give you, rather than appreciating them for all they did give, you will be unable to love your own inner child.

You are an adult now. It is your job to heal this inner child, not your parents' job. They did the best they could. They took you as far as they could, given the limitations of their relationships with their parents. When does the "buck of blame" stop? Now! It's high time we all forgave and forgot and set our parents free forever.

Setting your own creations free can be a challenging process. Even writing a book and releasing it through a publishing company to a world of readers requires a leap of faith. Letting go of an actual child into adulthood is a complex and gradual process, which works best when you are continually looking inwards to what your part in holding on is.

Many of us have a need to be needed, which often becomes confused with love itself. As long as you have someone dependent on you, you may feel like a useful human being, with something to offer. Letting go of this need will usually bring up your own real needs, which perhaps you were denying by attending to others.

Children come to parents in many different ways—some biological, some metaphysical. In the end you create them in your life no matter how they find you or you them. It's all natural! And the more you choose to give your all to all the children of your creation, the more you come to experience that we are all children of the Supreme Father (or Mother) and that there is a force in the universe that attends to us all.

DIVINE COMEDY

"Why is He smiling?"
"I guess He gets the joke."

I remember a joke. It went something like this: There was this vagabond who felt close to God all his life until one day he felt suddenly abandoned. He struggled and struggled from that day on, until finally he went to meet his Maker. God showed this man a video replay of his life, and he saw two sets of footprints crossing the desert until, at a very clear point, only one set continued. "You see!" said the indignant man to God. "That's where you left me. From that point on I had to do it alone!" God looked at the man and shook his head. "Don't be absurd. It was at that point you collapsed and I carried you the rest of the way."

That was the way I felt about God most of my life. I didn't know whether He was carrying me or had left me to my own devices. I was not brought up religious, and after my Bar Mitzvah I became more secular and less spiritual. For many years I fancied myself an existentialist, until someone pointed out that they were never happy, so I stopped being one. Then I became an academic, and God seemed to be a member of a club other than the one I belonged to. Certainly, He was never mentioned at any social gathering I attended. Once in a while, someone might have referred to Him as someone who had died. Later, I became a political activist and it was fashionable to think of God as a tool for oppression, a solace to the working people who needed a promise of heaven after death in order to justify killing themselves on earth. God is not popular among rebels, because if you're a true rebel at heart, you are opposed to all authority figures, and God seemed the best way to summon up all that resentment to Dad.

The less I believed in God, the more I seemed to notice His presence. It was easy for me to think God didn't live in New York City. If there was a God, surely He couldn't stand the pollution. When I began to travel, however, I couldn't help but see that there was a Presence in the universe that had never been explained in the classroom. I looked in the ocean, and I could see It move. I looked in the desert, and I could see Its constant stillness. I looked in the clear night sky, and I could see It shining everywhere. I looked at the redwood tree, and I could see Its splendor and majesty. Much as my intellect had been trained in objectivity, I could not deny there was a Mystery At Work that was far beyond the limits of the scientific method.

"Why is He smiling?"
"I guess He gets the joke."

I remember studying logic, when my teacher presented some philosopher's—I think it was Descartes'—proof that God exists. It went something like this: God, by definition, is that than which there is nothing greater; if God didn't exist, then there would be something greater, namely that than which there is nothing greater and which exists; therefore, God, by definition, must exist.

We had a fierce discussion in class about this logic, and it all centered around whether existence is better than non-existence, the very crux of the proof. I remember feeling that this was all very cold and calculating, and that if there were a God, surely He would not be so neatly categorized. I remembered Oscar Wilde, who said, "Consistency is the hobgoblin of small minds," and I thought that God would surely be Someone who transcended all the petty arguments of philosophers and other "little minds."

I can now see, however, what Descartes was getting at, in his own calculating way. Of course, existence is better than non-existence; in fact, existence is what we value as the greatest gift of all. If not, we'd all be committing suicide to get to something better, and I don't notice any long lines waiting to jump off the Washington Bridge.

Love, in a way, assumes God's presence. How can two people be in love if they don't participate in Something greater than each of their limited, separate identities? Being in love is being in a Beingness that transcends separation. Being in love is experiencing your own beingness as something far greater than you previously thought. Let's face it—love is the world's best peak experience, a taste of the immortal, a leap out of the survival part of our consciousness and into the eternal truths of life itself. Love is the sense of unity in diversity; pleasure is God's love in our bodies.

In most relationships, people take this taste of the divine and try to reduce it to the everyday world of need, obligation, and responsibility. In doing so, they often forget the spiritual source of love, and soon their material concerns have completely blinded their own divinity. Then they must leave the relationship in order to continue their spiritual quest. Love can only conquer all when you choose to bring the world of the mundane up to the world of the sublime, not the other way around. The real challenge for "romantic realists," as opposed to romantic escapists, is to experience their divine connection when they are at a supermarket or laundromat, as well as when watching a sunset in Maui or Mykonos.

Love is the point of contact, the experience of two parts of the universe feeling their oneness. People are terrified of love the way they are terrified of God; they don't want to lose their individuality by surrendering to something beyond their egos. They would rather stay in their separate cells than merge with the One, which feels like death. And so they hold on to their aloneness, their pain within, thinking it builds character and makes them special. Many people come to me defending their pain, almost proud of the fact that their pain is better than anyone else's. This is the tyranny of the ego, which wants to replace God as the object of worship in our hearts. Your defense system, your personal Pentagon, is the temple of this ego and must come tumbling down in order for love to flourish in your life.

"Why is He smiling?"
"I guess He gets the joke."

In all my previous relationships, God had never entered the picture. In my first marriage, a Ph.D. and tenure seemed like the surest ticket to heaven. In my second marriage creativity and acknowledgement seemed the key to the gates. Now, with Mallie, it was suddenly altogether different. God was so obviously there that to miss Him would have been to miss it all.

At first, however, His presence seemed awkward. We noticed Him, of course, this Presence larger than the sum of our individual parts, this Beingness greater than our egos. This Energy Field in which miracles became commonplace and God's will was so obviously our hearts' desires. He was kind of this Big Thing we lived in, loved in, laughed in, but at first It was too big to talk about. We just kind of nodded knowingly all the time, and went around knowing that everything was okay, that we were really happy, that there was never anything to worry about, that everything was, thank God, in His hands and that they were steady (unlike our obstetricians') and so we could relax and celebrate and tell everyone the good news.

More and more, we began to talk to Him. Her. It. We'd close our eyes and listen for the voice in our hearts, ask questions, get answers. Mallie began to read inspirational literature to me, then we began to write down our gratitudes regularly, and pray and practice forgiveness, and tithe to some spiritual source of inspiration. We went through the *Course In Miracles* together, as well as *The Door Of Everything*, *The Last Barrier*, *The Invisible Way*. These books, as well as others, seemed to open our minds to the experience of something beyond, some mysterious connective tissue in the universe. We began to melt down to our cores; present time became our favorite place to meet. And when our egos would roar and attempt to dominate and control, we had a larger context in which to hold our battles. It wasn't the books; it was something our relationship seemed to be receiving.

I realized that in all my past relationships I had been basically locked in my ego. I had always fallen in love, which felt more like falling from love, or falling from Grace. In the beginning, there was always a tremendous rush of good feeling, but it would be like an aphrodisiac, seducing me into an unconscious stupor. When I would later wake up, I'd discover that the love had vanished, and I was left with an emptiness in my gut. I never knew how to make love last. If God was love, He seemed like a trickster I couldn't trust.

Love seemed schizophrenic to me before Mallie. On the one hand it was infinite and eternal. No logical system could measure its size, shape, form, reasons. It was uncontainable joy and aliveness. It was fun. On the other hand, it seemed always to get reduced to mundane concerns, practicalities, obligations, resentments, and struggles. Looking back, I can now see that as long as I was blinded by the ego, I could not see the light. As long as I thought I was separate from God, all my relationships were founded in separation, and even if there was temporary escape from the solitude, ultimately the wall would rise and the loneliness replace the union. No amount of struggle could overcome this wall—which was in my mind—not *out there*. I could see how all the frustration would build into conflicts, trying to use all that energy it took to hold on to the wall to destroy it. It was paralyzing. Nothing short of divine intervention would help.

"Why is He smiling?"
"I guess He gets the joke."

If you believe you are separate and are waiting for what Leonard Orr calls "the divine meat axe" to fall, it is difficult to perceive your universe as safe, let alone pleasurable. Fear grips your body every step of the way. You live in fear of making mistakes, accidents befalling you, being in the wrong place or relationship at the wrong time. You constantly question everything. You judge everyone. Your survival seems to be based on mistrust, suspicion, and paranoia. Surrender feels like death. And the more you love someone and someone loves you, the more you are confronted with your own internal division. To trust or not to trust, that is the question!

Without God, you cannot take that leap of faith into something that's basically supportive and nurturing in the universe. Your fear holds you back. Since your thoughts are creative, the more you focus on your doubts, the more data you collect to prove the whole world is out to get you. The best that you can get to with a partner is: *it's you and me, babe, against the world*. But then the same thoughts that led you away from the world lead you away from each other. You have chosen solitude, and solitude is the home you return to. At least, that's the way it was for me.

With Mallie, the desire to surrender was almost always far greater than the fear of loss. Whereas in the past, my attitude had always been: *I'll see if this works out, then I'll choose it*, now my feeling was: *I chose this many lifetimes ago, it's time to stop running away from it and let it unfold*. And what unfolded was always so marvelous. We called our first business *Little Miracles* because we felt blessed with an ability to laugh and play and be happy together, and to share it with others. On the one hand we felt totally ordinary, not special at all. On the other hand we felt chosen to demonstrate to the world the possibilities for a long-lasting, Happy and Holy Romance.

God seemed to have given us this purpose, and when we were on purpose, we felt satisfied and happy. Sometimes, we strayed too far into work, and forgot to spend time alone together, or with the children. Whenever this would happen, everything would get crazy for a while—

until we took the time to nourish our roots, our connections at home. We learned the perfect balance between taking care of our own needs and serving the world, and that serving God was not always what our pictures looked like. We came to see that life is both expansion and contraction—a heart beats, cells pulsate, the whole universe is vibrating in and out, like breathing. We found that rhythm in our love for each other, and God would always correct us in mid-course when we drifted off-purpose.

> *"Why is He smiling?"*
> *"I guess He gets the joke."*

Perhaps we found God most of all in our own bed. The union we experienced could not be explained biologically. The sense of Oneness in the cells of our body was spiritual, as well as physical. We seemed to carry the knowledge of each other in our individual bodies, and this could not have been possible had we not both been surrendered to a higher form of energy than any one individual can experience. When we made love, we were much greater than the sum of our parts. And when we took this knowledge out into the world, the sense of Oneness possible in all relationships, at all times, at home as well as at work, became the major lesson we shared.

We would always remind people that they needed to go through their aloneness to get to the other side. Often people seek solace from their separateness, comfort in the midst of loneliness, and this can often rip you off. Going through the solitude cycle to its completion empowers you to be whole and self-sufficent. Stopping the process in mid-stream often just delays the final push. In the end, the deeper you surrender to yourself under all circumstances, the more you experience the perfection of the universe, and with that inevitably comes the spiritual awakening which allows union between apparently separate individuals. We are alone. And the one always leads to the One.

Before Mallie, I had always conceived of life—and all the things it contains—as having a beginning, a middle, and end. There seemed to be a built-in obsolescence factor governing the human body, relation-ships, cars, clothes. The whole planet seemed to be deteriorating like my teeth. Decay was the way of the world, I thought. With Mallie the love always drew me back to the present time. Instead of expecting the worst, I began to experience wonderful surprises as the norm. I felt an unlimited source of energy, love, and potential between us. And I felt safer than ever before to swim with the flow of life, not against it. I wasn't waiting to see how it worked out, I was too much in it to think about getting out. And it seemed so infinite there *was* no out. Being in it, time seemed to stop. In love there is no time, just eternal now-ness. In Australia, they call it "dreamtime," an endless interval of immortality available for surrendering. We came to God in the here-and-now, also His favorite place to rendezvous.

In Israel we felt all the layers of religious separation peel off us. We found peace from all the holy wars we had fought. We were left with a deep sense of overall oneness. In Greece we felt the passion of the gods, that spirituality was not separate from the real world, that God was not the glory of the past, but the Grace of the here-and-now, the Holy Instant. In Australia we felt that perfect paradise, that womb or garden of Eden we had mistakenly thought God tossed us out of. It was still there, in fact, heaven on earth as innocent as the day of creation, and all that we had to do to return to it was to let go of the thought that we had ever left it. It seemed clear to us that God had already done a perfect job, and that once we all awakened from the dream of imperfection, we would all choose to be together again and see that there was more than enough for everyone once we tapped the infinite.

"Why is He smiling?"
"I guess He gets the joke."

The internal debate continued in my mind for a long time. How could I trust God when He let children starve to death, Jews get gassed, and Vietnam happen? Surely, if there were some beneficent force in the universe, It would not tolerate such injustice. I could feel how much I resented God for giving me freedom, although I valued freedom next to life itself. However, I could also see how what sometimes seemed like forces of destruction, like a brush fire or an earthquake, were just the creative forces of the universe working in their own perfect way, but which man was not in harmony with. I came to see that when I surrendered to life, there was no positive or negative, just life itself. Only in my separation was there any conflict. And I had to admit how all apparent injustices were created by the victim as well as the victimizer, how every so-called crime was an unconscious complicity among all the parties. I began to forgive God, forgive myself for thinking I was separate. I wrote the affirmations:

I am now willing for my ego to fail so I can experience more of God's success.

I am willing to see the God in everyone, whether or not they fit my pictures of God.

Since God is the unknown, the more I know I don't know, the closer I feel to God.

And as the drama of separation left my heart and the illusion of separation left my world, I could see that Mallie and I were just parts of each other. We were so much a part of each other, in fact, that we could never really be apart, no matter where our bodies were on this planet. We would go to separate cities to work, at times, and still feel the Oneness connecting us. We both realized that in love there was a connection beyond any disagreement, a sameness beyond every difference, and how unity through diversity was how God manifested His presence.

Energy moved in mysterious ways. But there was a sense to it all, a fundamental purpose, a unifying principle at work, which could be seen in each part as well as the whole.

In studying our relationship, we learned how to perceive the entire universe. In studying the entire universe, we learned how to perceive our relationship.

There were many collective thoughts of separation, conflict, inequality, oppression, war, and doom one could buy into. But the less these thoughts seemed part of our own survival mechanisms, the less juice we experienced in their presence. And when we did get activated, we told the truth as fast as we could and let our passion for peace, balance, and harmony carry us back to the center.

All of life began to look like one big divine comedy. Which is not to say that we lost compassion for people who suffered. In fact, we just lost the guilt, the idea that we were to blame for the woes of others. In releasing the guilt, the separation vanished too, and that's when the compassion really took over.

And so we could see the comedy and feel the hurt. If God was laughing at the drama unfolding, why couldn't we join the chorus?

We had cried enough for one universe.

"Why is He smiling?"
"I guess He gets the joke."

I remember once in the early days of our relationship, I came out into the living room one morning and looked about. At that time I gave a lot of seminars in the living room and we had this big blackboard against the wall. This particular morning, when I looked at the blackboard, there was an illustration that brought a smile to my face. There was a simple, child-like drawing of Christ on the Cross. The unusual thing about the picture was that Christ had a big smile across his face. Suzie had drawn it. She was eight at the time.

Mallie and I looked at this drawing all day. It somehow seemed to symobolize how we felt. Life was not about suffering, martyrdom, and crucifixion. That was the drama, the great human soap opera. The truth was in happy endings. The resurrection was a happy ending.

Living happily ever after is not the end of a fairy tale. It is the common purpose that all life seeks.

"Why is He smiling?"

God is not a relic, not an obsolete concept that made sense in simpler days but is now meaningless and useless. On the contrary, God is, more than ever, an idea whose time has come.

I read recently in a popular science magazine that a group of top scientists and theologians had gathered in order to redefine God for the 21st century. They discussed various ideas of God, the problems of an increasingly technological society, and how to bring spiritual and scientific values into greater harmony. Eventually, they settled on a definition of God that was acceptable and sensible for them all: God is the principle of simplicity and unity that seems to be underneath all the complexity at the surface of things.

Lovers are always searching for this simple unity in their relationship. Often, the complications of modern life seem to be opposed to spiritual union, leading lovers further and further away from the so-called "real" world. This is the fallacy of Romeo and Juliet and all the great romantic escapists. They choose their love over the world, death over life, and their love becomes the supreme expression of the absence of God in their lives.

The alternative to this madness is what I call "romantic realism," a philosophy that encourages lovers to be open to the possibilities for experiencing romance at all times in their relationships. The divine is always available; it does not need any special circumstances in order to manifest. When we are willing to see the ordinary in an extraordinary light, miracles become commmonplace. Any true quest leads you back to life, not away from it.

Next time you pay your telephone bill, thank God for the communication He provides. Next time you are in a supermarket, thank God for His eternal nourishment. Next time you wash dishes, praise God for the water. You and your lover can be in a state of bliss, no matter where you are or what you are doing. Once you open the door, the light comes flooding in!

TWO HEARTS ARE BETTER THAN ONE!

Two hearts *are* better than one! The purpose of all relationships, no matter what the temporary difficulties, is to make one's life easier. We are one human family of interdependent human beings. The human ecology of this planet depends on our willingness to rediscover a spirit of cooperation, rather than competition. We need to see ourselves as one team, rather than competing teams.

Aligning the human family is a one-by-one process. First you align yourself with God, then a mate, children, colleagues, friends, and eventually, each new person you meet. In my relationship with Mallie, I have made my life easier—emotionally, mentally, and physically. I have learned, and I continue to learn, to let go of the rebellion that keeps me separate, while at the same time acknowledging the differences that make us each unique. I now have a direct experience of oneness through diversity that can support me in all my other relationships.

In the past, I would resist the lessons I had clearly attracted into my life in order to grow. With Mallie I have learned to surrender to the purity of the process, not run away, to face myself more deeply than ever. Your partner is a divine mirror of your divine self. It is impossible to find yourself by yourself. If you were to shut yourself up in a cave and meditate for 1,000 years, you'd still have to come out one day and face the light of the world. Your partner is how you come face to face with yourself. How you see the people you love the most is as close as you come to seeing yourself. We all have blind spots, shadows that cover ourselves and prevent us from seeing ourselves fully. When you find someone who loves you unconditionally, that love will burn off the shadows and bring you into full light. The only thing that makes this hard is when we are afraid to come out of the cave. Once you choose, you discover the joy and aliveness you have kept secret for so long.

* * * * *

I was doing a meditation, which turned into a past life regression. Images, thoughts, memories and dreams raced across my mind. I wasn't worrying whether or not they were real, because I was searching for an image from the dark, distant recesses of my own being, some picture of my relationship with Mallie at the very beginning of our choice to be together. I saw us in Russia, and in France, and during the Middle Ages, and in ancient Greece. And as my imagination regressed through all of evolution, the scenes raced by faster than I could see them all. Then, suddenly, it slowed down, and one picture burst through clear as day.

Mallie and I were two fish, neon green fish with black and yellow iridescent eyes, swimming side by side in some ancient sea. Everything was astoundingly peaceful. We had to swim side by side in order to see each other, because our big black and yellow eyes were on the sides of our heads. It must have been then that we chose to take parallel paths in all of our lives. We had chosen to be side by side. And we continue to do so!

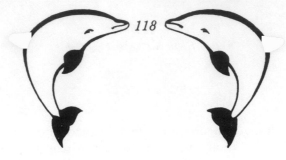

P ♥ A ♥ R ♥ T

2

CREATE-
A-
MATE

*How To
Attract And Sustain
Your Perfect Loving Relationship*

CREATE-
A-
MATE

Many people read "how-to-do-it" books these days. There are books on how to fix your car, how to build your house, how to run a small business—to mention a few. But when it comes to the business of constructing a perfect loving relationship, people seem to be much more skeptical that such a thing can be designed.

Yet you have always designed your relationships, whether you know it or not. Your thoughts are creative, and your thoughts about relationships, based largely on conclusions you made watching your parents and siblings relate to each other and to you, become unconscious patterns that produce repetitive, compulsive behavior in your relationships. That is why you find yourself in similar situations, feeling similar feelings, with different people. You unconsciously project what is unresolved within your own mind onto your partner in any relationship. This is why people who insist upon "flowing with it," rather than being conscious of it, are often giving their unconscious programming a chance to have a field day.

Of course your thoughts are creative. If you want to stand up, you must think about it on some level. If you want to build a house, you must conceive of it first, plan it on paper. Moreover, if your conception is faulty, how can its realization be anything but flawed. It's the same with relationships. If your whole idea of what you want, expect, or think you deserve is limited, then your resulting relationship is bound to be full of shortcomings. The perfect execution of a misconceived plan is doomed to failure.

Conscious conception is an essential first step in creating a conscious relationship! You've *fallen* in love enough! It's time to stop falling, stop expecting your Knight in Shining Armor to come along, swoop you up, and rescue you from the cold, cruel world. It's time to stop looking for a parental surrogate, who will allow you to be the child you always wanted to be, who will take care of you, provide for you, and carry you through life so you never have to stand on your own two feet. It's time to stop *falling*. It's time for Romantic Realism.

A relationship goes through a life cycle that is largely the projection of two individual life cycles. So let's start at the beginning, the conception of your ideal loving relationship.

STEP 1: The Shopping List

Your thoughts are creative. You are not a victim. Acknowledge that whatever you created in the past, you had the power to create it, and you can use that same creative power to attract something better right now. If you're single, you can create a mate. If you're with someone, you can transform what you have into your ideal.

Most people conceive of their relationships unconsciously, stumbling into one, bumping into another and crashing into a third. They don't know it, but they are unconsciously attracting people by the power of their unconscious mind, patterns, preconceptions and expectations that literally draw substance to them. A woman with an alcoholic father attracts an alcoholic man. A man with a suffocating mother unconsciously draws to him a dominating woman. And so it goes . . .

. . . until you finally wake up from the dream and choose to be aware of the quality of your own consciousness about relationships. The Shopping List is just what it sounds like. You take out a piece of paper and write on the top of the page: MY IDEAL LOVING RELATION-SHIP. Then you make a list of all those qualities you most want in a relationship. Be very specific. This is your order to the universe, and the universe always says, *YES!* And there is no lack in the universe. So let go of the thought that there is only one one-and-only out there for you. There are an abundance of people with whom you can create your ideal. This is a much more positive context in which to attract your mate.

So make your list of the kind of man or woman you want. List all the physical, spiritual, mental, emotional, financial, cultural qualities you like the best. Don't leave anything out. Once a woman made this list but forgot to put she wanted an "available" man—you guessed it, she attracted and fell in love with a married man. Another time, someone forgot to put "age" down, and attracted a perfect partner, but he was 80 years old.

When you're done with your list (you can change it or add to it as you go), on the bottom of the page write: *THIS OR SOMETHING BETTER NOW COMES TO ME, IN EASY AND PLEASURABLE WAYS, WITH GOOD TO ALL CONCERNED. THANK YOU, GOD.*

MY IDEAL LOVING RELATIONSHIP:

_____

_____

_____

_____

_____

_____

_____

_____

_____

_____

_____

_____

_____

_____

_____

_____

_____

_____

_____

_____

There are two implants, or affirmations, you should work with in conjunction with your list. An implant is a positive thought you plant in the garden of your subconscious mind in order to produce a desired result. You write each 20 times a day with a response column on the right hand side of the page. You draw a line down the middle of the page, and focus your energy on the implant, not the response, which is like a weed you need to uproot so your new idea has breathing room.

1. *I now attract my ideal loving relationship*—namely, your shopping list.
2. *The divine plan of my relationship now manifests!*

Other thoughts you want to immerse yourself in are:
I am a beautiful, lovable person. I deserve to be loved.
There is always an abundance of attractive, available men (women) around me.
I am a powerful magnet. I can attract what I want.

Write the affirmations given above:

_____

_____

_____

_____

_____

_____

_____

_____

_____

_____

_____

STEP 2: The Treasure Map

A Treasure Map is a visual tool for manifesting specific results in your life. Get a large piece of poster board on which you will paste words and images respresenting your ideal loving relationship. Go through old magazines and cut out any pictures, phrases, and sentiments that illustrate the qualities you most want to attract.

The theme should be perfect, romantic partnership, and should include all aspects of your relationship—physical, mental and spiritual. Perhaps have two romantic lovers embracing, with a photograph of you superimposed over the appropriate figure you're pasting up.

Also, have a symbol of God on your map, a representation of the divine connection through which we manifest. And include the implants, *This or something better now manifests itself for me, in easy and totally satisfying ways, with good to all concerned,* and *I now receive assistance and cooperation from all those necessary to bring about my desired result, thank you God!*

Assemble your Treasure Map and hang it in a private place, where you can meditate on it daily.

Treasure Maps are a proven method for clearing your mind on what it wants to attract, then actually attracting it to you. I have witnessed many people create their perfect home, car, job, vacation, and relationship with the help of such maps. If you are a visual person especially, treasure maps, in association with written affirmations, can produce rapid results in your life.

These steps create the conscious conception of your relationship. When the conception is murky, the life of a relationship is misguided from the start. Getting clear on what you want enables you to recognize it when it comes along, an important step when you realize that you will now be attracting what is basically unfamiliar to you!

STEP 3: Complete The Past

The energy you use to hold on to the past is the same energy you need to create your future. Moreover, the extent to which you cling to the past is the extent to which you are blocked in receiving what you truly want.

Clean up the past. Start with your parents. Set them free! Forgive them completely! Love them unconditionally, as they are, without any hope of ever changing them. See them as perfect the way they are! Take responsibility for what you created with them! Focus on the things you love about them! Write "letters of completion" to them, whether they are alive or dead. Start with a statement like, "My purpose in writing this letter is to let go of anything between me and loving you fully, and to express my gratitude to you for all you have given and taught me. . ." Rewrite the letters as many times as necessary until they are just right. Do not mail them until they are in a form that you would not mind receiving, if someone you loved sent them to you.

Do this same process with your siblings.

And make a list of all your other major incomplete relationships. A good way to know if they are incomplete is to imagine the person walking into the room and notice whether you feel totally comfortable in his or her presence. Include in your list any former lovers, friends, bosses, partners, and other significant people in your life. Write one letter after another until you are complete with everyone, having released them lovingly to their destiny and yourself to yours.

Let go of all the resentment and grievances. What you have not forgiven these people for—especially your parents—is what you will tend to blame your partners for. If you need to speak to anyone in person, do so. Pray for release, if that helps. You need to clear your internal space completely to be open to the wonderful surprises coming to you.

Sometimes it is even advisable to "fire" your parents. Call them up or write to them and tell them their job as parents is now complete, you are fully grown and can take care of yourself, and you would now like to transform your relationship from parent/child to friend/friend. In all likelihood, they will be relieved to learn that you have made it. They can relax.

If you are incomplete in mourning, complete it! People hold on to past pain from the loss of a loved one as though it were their only connection left. It's not true. When you release the grief, the unconditional love remains, the true essence of the bond emerges, and you might even deepen your psychic connection by letting go of the physical loss.

RELATIONSHIPS I NEED TO COMPLETE:

_____

_____

_____

_____

_____

_____

_____

_____

_____

_____

Completion Checklist:

☐ PARENTS   ☐ PARTNERS

☐ SIBLINGS   ☐ OTHERS

☐ FORMER LOVERS   ☐ _____

☐ FRIENDS   ☐ _____

☐ BOSSES   ☐ _____

STEP 4: *Prepare Yourself!*

In addition to preparing your inner self for your partner, prepare your external space as well. Get rid of any items, momentos, and souvenirs from old relationships, including photographs, jewelry, or gifts of any kind that represent a bond to that person. If you owe an old mate money, handle the debt. If he has left articles of clothing in your house, send them back to him or give them to the Salvation Army. Nostalgia for the past is a subtle enemy of the future.

Clean out your closet, your dresser and your desk. Handling your external space handles your internal space. A good spring cleaning every once in a while does the trick. I once saw a T-shirt that read, *If you want to clean up the world, start with your own room!*

THINGS I NEED TO DO TO PREPARE MYSELF:

STEP 5: *Be Aware of Your Patterns!*

A pattern is a form of unconscious behaviour that you act out compulsively. Some common patterns are: leaving before you are left, being abandoned, helplessness, struggle, revenge, incestuous energy, guilt, and specific family patterns you've acquired by imitating your parents.

You can unravel your patterns by looking at your repetitive results in life. If you keep attracting men without money, why? If women always leave you for other men, why? If you always attract a partner who is physically sick, why?

There are always clear reasons why you attract the person you do. Either it's someone who is reflecting those qualities in one or both of your parents that you're incomplete with, or else you're playing the part of your parent, and your partner is behaving the way you did in the presence of your parent.

You can discover which thoughts are producing which results in your life by doing a little "self-interrogation" process, where you write on the top of the page, *The reason I created* _____*is* . . . and list the thoughts that come up spontaneously. When you hit a thought that feels powerful in your body, it's probably the limiting one. Breathe it out. Use an affirmation to express the opposite point of view.

You can free yourself of patterns if you take responsibility for creating them in the first place. You must accept the fact that you have chosen a particular course of action because (1) your parents did it, so it seemed right; (2) it was in rebellion against your parents, so it seemed right; (3) you picked it up unconsciously along the way and didn't even know what you were doing.

Indeed, the first step in releasing a negative pattern is to know what you're doing, to become conscious of what was previously unconscious behavior.

The second step is to experience how addicted to this form of behavior you are and how it seems like a basic survival mechanism of your personality.

The third and final step is to choose out of the pattern by saying *no* to it over and over again. If your pattern is struggle, you must develop the pattern of ease in your life by practicing pleasure.

MY PATTERNS ARE:

The reason I created _____ is:

_____

_____

_____

The reason I created _____ is:

_____

_____

_____

The reason I created _____ is:

_____

_____

_____

The reason I created _____ is:

_____

_____

_____

For each pattern, consider how addicted to it you are. Now create a new pattern of ease by releasing the addiction and saying NO to it.

Notes:

_____

_____

_____

_____

_____

_____

_____

_____

_____

_____

_____

_____

_____

_____

_____

_____

_____

_____

_____

_____

STEP 6: *Pleasure Process*

Make a list of your ten favorite pleasures. Put a check next to any pleasure you experienced regularly in your most recent, significant relationship. Commit yourself to more pleasure in your own life, and schedule your pleasures into your daily calendar as frequent activities. If you can't pleasure yourself by yourself, nobody else will do it for you.

MY 10 FAVORITE PLEASURES:

☐ 1. _____

☐ 2. _____

☐ 3. _____

☐ 4. _____

☐ 5. _____

☐ 6. _____

☐ 7. _____

☐ 8. _____

☐ 9. _____

☐ 10. _____

STEP 7: *Primal Law*

Your Primal Law is your most negative thought about yourself, thoughts like, *I'm unwanted, I'm not good enough, I'm bad, There's something wrong with me, I'm ugly, I always hurt the people I love,* or *My love causes separation!*

These are conclusions we make from birth about ourselves in relationships. Since your thoughts are creative, the most primal thoughts—being the ones you've thought the longest—are the most influential in your relationships.

For example, if your Primal Law is *I'm not good enough,* and your partner's is *I always hurt the people I love,* don't be surprised if you experience your partner hurting you, by disapproving, betraying, or leaving. In a relationship, since love brings up anything unlike itself, eventually two people will experience their Laws at work. If they are not conscious enough to know what's going on, their relationship could end right there.

Usually we overcompensate for our Primal Laws. If you think you hurt people, you might decide to go into a helping profession like teaching, medicine, or social work to compensate. If you think you're ugly, you might become an artist and create beauty. If you think your love causes separation, you might become the peace-maker in other people's relationships. But even if you're stuck in overcompensating for your Primal Law, it will come back and haunt you when you least expect it.

Take out a piece of paper and write down your five most negative thoughts about yourself. Look for those thoughts that seem most basic to all your compulsive behavior in life. Then underline the single thought that seems at the root of the others. For example, if your list reads:

> 1) Men leave me
> 2) I'm too fat
> 3) I'm boring
> 4) I'm never good enough
> 5) Life is a struggle

Then *I'm never good enough* would be your law because if you're never good enough, you're not good enough to hold on to a man, to be thin, to be exciting, to have it easy.

My 5 Most Negative Thoughts About Myself:

1. _____

2. _____

3. _____

4. _____

5. _____

So, My Primal Law Is:

_____

_____

_____

Then you transform your Primal Law into your Eternal Law. Your Primal Law is the biggest lie you have told yourself, which seems like the truth. Your Eternal Law is the greatest truth about yourself, but it may seem like a lie at first—because you've been believing the negative so long.

Samples of Primal/Eternal Law conversions:

1. I'm not good enough   =   I'm perfect just the way I am
2. I can't make it   =   I've got it made
3. I hurt people   =   I am a pleasure to be with
4. I don't belong   =   I am a part of God's plan
5. I'm unwanted   =   I am a gift of God

My Primal/Eternal Law Conversion Is:

1. _____   =   _____

Write your Eternal Law as one of your daily implants. Write it 20 times a day until you embody it, feel it and experience it in all areas of your life.

Mastering your Eternal Law is building the foundation for an eternally happy loving relationship.

STEP 8: Self Esteem

Immersing yourself in your 10 favorite pleasures and Eternal Law are two ingredients in building high self-esteem.

Your relationship with yourself is the most important one in your life. Not only do people treat you the way you treat yourself, but you're the one you always have to live with.

If you can't make yourself happy, nobody else will be able to do it for you, at least not for very long. If you don't believe you deserve an extraordinary relationship, you'll never create it. If you don't love yourself, you will tend to attract other people who don't think much of themselves, and two empty cups can hardly fill each other up.

Of course, once in a while you might attract someone who loves you more than you love yourself, but if you do, you won't be able to receive the love. You'll think the other person is lying and begin to mistrust, pull away from, or reject him.

Most people are walking examples of the old Groucho Marx joke, "I wouldn't want to belong to any club that would have me for a member." With an attitude like that, how can you attract, much less surrender, to a perfect loving relationship?

Having high self esteem is natural and not egotistical. An egoist really loathes himself but pretends he's God's gift to the world. A person with high self esteem thinks the world of himself, is grateful to God, and wants to share his gifts with others.

Creating high self esteem is easy if you follow the guidelines below:

1) Keep a book of successes by your bed and every night, before you go to sleep, write down 5 successes, no matter how minor, you had that day. Build a SUCCESS CONSCIOUSNESS.

2) Let other people's praise sink in. If someone acknowledges you for something, don't dismiss it as meaningless, think "Bullshit!" or discount it by thinking, "If they only really knew me . . ." Just take a breath and say, "Thank you!" You deserve praise and acknowledgment.

3) Enjoy your career! How many of your 10 favorite pleasures do you experience at work? Pleasure and work are not incompatible. In fact, truly successful people enjoy their work so much you can hardly get them away from it. So add pleasure to your current job, or else create a more pleasurable one. You spend a good part of your life at work, and if work is a struggle, you bring pain and frustration home to your relationship each night. You've struggled enough!

4) Be lazy once in a while. You don't always have to do everything. You might be in the habit of thinking you never do enough, therefore being

a workaholic. Do nothing for a while. Appreciate yourself for who you are, not just what you do. Get into pure existence as your ultimate value, because love is a quality of existence, not action.

5) Love your body, which after all is the most visible part of yourself. Stand in front of a full-length mirror, naked, and acknowledge yourself for as long as you can each day, or at least several times a week. Look at yourself and say out loud, "I love my body, and so do others!" Stop looking into mirrors only to see what's wrong with you. Look for what's right. What you focus on expands.

6) If you make a mistake, don't criticize yourself. Simply learn the lesson and move on. Disapproving of yourself creates resentment and struggle. Forgiving yourself, learning the lesson, and moving on is the way to go.

7) Buy yourself the things you really love, not what you think you can afford. Get in the habit of giving yourself the best. Make sure, for example, you aren't buying clothes to conform to your parents or to rebel from them, but to express your unique magnificence.

8) Write yourself love notes, postcards, letters, and send them to yourself as reminders of how much you have going for you.

9) Together with your Eternal Law, work with 2 or 3 of the following implants:

a— I am highly pleasing to myself.
b— I am highly pleasing to myself in the presence of others.
c— I love myself unconditionally.
d— I forgive myself completely.
e— I deserve the best.
f— I am great! God don't make junk!
g— I have everything I need to get everything I want.
h— I am a beautiful, lovable man (woman). I deserve to be loved.

Generally it is best to write no more than 3 affirmations, 20 times each day, for three weeks.

Rewrite Your Eternal Law Here:

_____

_____

Now, Select 2 or 3 of the Implants and Write Them Here:

_____

_____

_____

_____

_____

_____

_____

_____

_____

_____

_____

_____

Over the next three weeks, take a blank sheet of paper each day, and write down each affirmation 20 times.

STEP 9: Be Alone!

As the final preparation for creating your ideal mate, be alone! Don't cover up your loneliness with casual, meaningless affairs, which in the end leave you more empty than you were. Take the bull by the horns and wrestle your loneliness to the ground. Be celibate for a while. Get out of your addiction to sex. Get out of thinking you need other people to make you happy. When you learn to be happy by yourself, you are in the perfect space to attract someone else who can be happy alone. Two people who can be happy alone can be doubly happy together. Their cups are full and continually spilling over each other.

Get REBIRTHED during this time. Rebirthing is the most powerful and pleasurable process for getting in touch with your own personal power, perfection and love, as well as releasing all those primal patterns in the way of your happiness.

STEP 10: Take Risks

When you feel whole and full within, you are ready to attract your perfect partner. You must, however, be willing to take chances. When you meet people, ask for what you want. Be willing to say yes when you mean yes and no when you mean no. Be able to take no for an answer and move on. We all have a "rejection quota." When we are rejected enough, we stop rejecting ourselves and that's when others start accepting us.

If you're a woman, you might want to be more assertive in asking men out. Nowadays, men tend to shy away from asking women out because they don't want to come on to them and risk a furious response. If you want equality in your relationship, start at the beginning and realize that it is now appropriate for either sex to do the initiating.

STEP *11*: *Do What You Enjoy Doing*

People often become unnatural in their search for a partner. They begin to do things they don't really enjoy doing, thinking that they must in order to meet people. So they go to singles bars, which they hate, or to parties they don't want to be at. And they look for someone else who doesn't want to be there to take them home.

If you think about it, it is far more likely that you will meet a compatible partner doing the things you love. If you enjoy a museum, go to it. If you love the beach, go there. If you enjoy jogging, skiing, walking in the park, do those things. That's where you'll meet other people who enjoy the same things as you. Moreover, if you don't meet someone, at least you'll be having a good time by yourself.

This is so obvious that most people forget it.

THINGS I REALLY ENJOY DOING:

_____

_____

_____

_____

_____

_____

_____

_____

_____

_____

_____

_____

_____

STEP *12*: *Keep Your Eyes Open*

Since you are now looking for someone who doesn't fit your pictures or patterns, you need to train your eyes to see the unexpected. For example, if you've had a struggle pattern all your life, you probably avoided partners who were easy, who loved you for no reason at all, who were not a challenge. You were attracted to those tough cases whom you could work hard on, rehabilitate, change, improve. You struggled with partners worth the effort—or were they?

Now, on your SHOPPING LIST, you've asked the universe to send you someone totally different, easy, relaxed, and together. When you meet such a person, you will not be accustomed to him or her; your mind will be accustomed to the tough ones. So look carefully, take a breath, and be willing to see the attraction if it's there.

STEP *13*: *Friendship First*

All good loving relationships are based on friendship. And it is far easier to evolve a loving sexual relationship from a friendship than the other way around. Moreover, if the basis of friendship is established first, then you will always be able to fall back on it when other areas of your relationship have problems.

Don't rush into sexual involvement. What's the hurry? You're worth waiting for. I know a teacher who recommends that new couples do 90 days of celibacy before they become too involved. This both clears the couple's sexual aura and gives ample time for getting to know each other. I'm not saying 90 days is essential, but a few weeks wouldn't hurt anything.

Take your time. You can have physical affection without sex. I know many people who sleep with friends without having sex. Always be clear on what serves your higher purpose, what you want in the long run. And say no to what you don't want and yes to what you really desire. Don't fall into the trap of—*if I don't make love with him now, he'll leave me.* You're worth getting to know. And wooing is part of the pleasure of loving.

On the other hand, if you have a pattern of non-involvement, if you're always saving yourself for Mister Right, it might be time to practice being in relationships rather than saving yourself for some imaginary one-and-only. In the area of love, practice makes perfect, and until you give yourself, you won't find yourself.

The important thing is to strike the right balance between your new consciousness about relationships and certain valid old-fashioned virtues, like waiting and wooing and saving yourself and not rushing in

Remember, love is not blind, nor is it something you want to fall into without thinking. Fools rush in. Wise men take a breath.

STEP 14: *Beginning To Be Together*

People often come to me or write to me in order to thank me for the work I've done with them. Sometimes they'll say something like: *Well, I've got my relationship now*—as though a relationship were a possession you can have, measure, and hold. Not so. Once you find your perfect partner, you must be equally conscious as when you conceived of him.

The beginning of being together is usually a critical time when the habits of your relationship are formed. You're often feeling so many wonderful loving feelings at the beginning that you tend to deny, neglect, or ignore "the other things." You're better off keeping your eyes open at this point.

Tell the truth fast! Sit down opposite each other, choose an A and a B, and each take a few minutes to communicate your fears to each other.

A. *A fear I have of being in love with you is* . . .
B. *Thank you.*

It's important that B only say thank you, and not try to handle or comfort A's fears. Let him or her get them out without discussion.

And get in the habit of telling each other your darkest thoughts right from the start.

Often, it is best to put your worst foot forward first in a relationship—to share all the worst things about yourself you're afraid you'll be rejected for down the road. This way, if your partner accepts and loves you unconditionally, you'll know you never have to hide in the relationship in the future.

STEP *15: Joint Implant*

Create a joint implant to affirm the qualities in your relationship that you want to expand. Have a rule: whenever one partner begins to say this thought aloud, the other must join in. Even if you're feeling totally resistant, you join in this higher thought to overcome your separation. The implant should be long enough so it is hard to hold on to any negative thoughts by the time you're done.

Bob and Mallie now have and enjoy ever-increasing love, health, happiness, wealth, wisdom, harmony, full self-expression, luxurious living spaces, easy and pleasurable travels and sexual bliss.

You can create your own.

OUR JOINT IMPLANT:

_____

_____

_____

_____

_____

_____

_____

_____

_____

_____

STEP 16: *I Love You!*

"I love you" are the most powerful three words I know. Usually, at the beginning of a relationship people can't stop telling each other, "I love you!" Then, as the days move into weeks and months, the verbal acknowledgment of love is put on the back burner and the unconscious patterns come up, and pretty soon the negativity seems more real than the love.

You can never tell someone you love "I love you" too many times. And the more you affirm the love when you do feel it, the more love you will generate to feel. Focus on the love!

STEP 17: *No Family Obligations*

It is best, especially early in a relationship, to have no family obligations to each other's family. When you first come together, you are the seed for a new family unit, and like any seed you need time, patience, space, and love to grow. It's enough of a challenge to surrender to your partner without bringing in too many other relatives too soon. Moreover, this gives each of you the opportunity to let go of your families a little more and become your own parent in your own life.

Allow your relationships with each other's parents and siblings to grow organically, not artificially. This way the bond among all of you will be chosen, real, and lasting.

STEP 18: *Choosing a Form*

Remember, love is essentially formless. It can neither be contained nor possessed. It is like a river. You can never put your foot in the same water twice—it's always flowing, continuously transforming.

The basis of a healthy relationship is when two people are each committed to their own personal well-being as well as to the well-being of the other. Each partner honors his own joy and aliveness while respecting his partner's as well. *This is the seed for an eternal loving relationship.*

The eternal nature of love is, of course, timeless, immeasurable, and uncontainable. If you choose to put this eternal love in a limited form, never lose sight of the eternal context that makes it work. If you want an ''open'' sexual form for your formless love, be sure you're not just acting compulsively, rebelling from your parents' way, church conditioning, or running an incest pattern. If your partner wants it open and you want it closed, figure out why you attracted someone out of harmony with your heart's desires. Is it your unavailable father or mother you've re-created? In the end you might have to choose between what you really want and your addiction to what you don't want.

If you have a fear of commitment, which usually originates in the feeling of ''no-exit terror'' from birth, you'll want to get rebirthed frequently until you connect with your internal freedom, which is not a function of external agreements. If you have a fear of abandonment, also rebirth the past memories out of your body so you will not be at the affect of this fear in your current relationship.

When your desire to surrender is greater than either your fear of loss or entrapment, your relationship is bound to succeed.

You can make agreements as to what form suits your purpose best. An agreement is an arrangement for a course of action you're both willing to be accountable for. Agreements are intended to serve you; you shouldn't be a slave to your agreements. They can be renegotiated if they no longer suit your purpose. Agreements should always be made for limited periods of time.

A commitment is more than an agreement. You make an agreement from your mind. You discover your commitment in your heart. And your natural commitment to someone you trust and desire to be with will always provide a strength and certainty that agreements can never provide. As you clear away the stuff between you and total surrender, you will notice your agreements naturally evolving into commitment, and then your commitment developing into devotion, where you are totally surrendered even to your commitment.

The purpose of playing with agreed-on forms is to develop enough trust to take the leap together.

STEP 19: *Games*

There is a series of games you can play with your partner to enhance your connection and dissolve separation.

1. "The Right Day Game":

You and your partner alternate being *right* for 24 hours each. This is a wonderful game if you have an issue of right and wrong in your relationship. Everyone is always right in his own mind, because his thoughts are creative and he will always attract the appropriate evidence to confirm his point of view. So right and wrong is absurd, but nevertheless it comes up. When your partner is right for a day, it does not mean you are wrong. It means you get to choose to be right too. You just agree with your partner whenever there is an issue that comes up during the day, be it what movie to see, what direction to turn in the car, or what to eat for dinner. Keep doing this process until the whole issue of right and wrong disappears. You will laugh a lot once you get into it, and you will come to appreciate how brilliant your partner often is. You will know you're complete with this game when you realize that it doesn't matter who's right or wrong, because if your partner has the highest thought, you're the first one he'll share it **with.** Your relationship can be a clear channel for inspirational ideas, once you get your individual egos out of the way.

2. "The Wet Truth Game":

Communication is the key to the door of unconditional love. In a relationship you want to feel free to express yourself without disapproval, and you want your partner to have the same safe space. Every night before you go to bed, fill up the tub and both get in. You then each get equal time to communicate any withholds from the day, positive or negative, without discussion or response. (The need to respond is often based on self-defense, and peace, remember, needs no defense.) this is an opportunity to catch up on each other's thoughts, as well as to release those petty negative thoughts that tend to snowball into major resentments if you don't get them out. Choose an A and a B, and it goes something like this:

A: Something I'd like to communicate to you is . . .
   I love you.
B: Thank you.
A: Something I'd like to communicate to you is . . .
   I didn't like it that you didn't wash your dishes this morning.
B: Thank you.
A: Something I'd like to communicate to you is . . .
   I was delighted that you called my mother today.
B: Thank you.
A: Something I'd like to communicate to you is . . .
   I resented your making a dinner date without asking me.
B: Thank you.

And keep going until you get it all out. In the Bible it says, "Never let the sun set on your anger!" Let go of it all. It's all just thoughts, which is why B does not respond. The purpose here is not discussion, but just the creation of a free space to say what's on your mind and let it go.

I recommend that you breathe well while doing this, and that when you're done you get out of the tub and let the water run down the drain, along with all the negativity you released.

3. **"The 24 Hour Contact Game":**
   When the forces of separation are up in your relationship, this is a fabulous game for reasserting your will to be together. You will need to play this game when you least want to, so take a breath and choose the higher road. The game is just what it sounds like: For 24 hours you and your partner maintain physical contact. Don't let anyone or anything come between you or pull you apart. If the phone rings, go together to answer it. If one goes to the bathroom, the other goes. And so forth and so on. You want to play this game as often as necessary, until you experience harmony in your choice to be together.

4. **"The Whole Bed Game":**
   Often a couple has a king-size bed, but each partner only experiences half of it. This can be symbolic of the separation in the relationship, where each person owns his 50%, but not the other half. Switching sides of the bed can open the door to owning the whole relationship, as well as the bed. Moreover, you will find yourself entering your partner's dreams, experiencing his aura and sexuality and thereby strengthening the psychic connection between you. This is just a simple game with profound results. Try it!

5. **"The Co-Isolation Game"**:

This is another game designed to enhance your spiritual bond, as well as let go of separation. You agree to spend 24 hours in isolation in adjacent rooms. You each keep a journal during this time. You also plan a schedule of things to think about at given times. Start with simple things. At noon you both think of a color for one minute, then write down the color. At one o'clock one partner thinks of a color for a minute and the other tries to receive it. At two, both partners think of a place. At three, one partner thinks of a place and the other tries to receive it. At four both partners think of a person you both know. At five one partner thinks of a person and the other tries to receive it. Plan out your schedule in advance, and keep a complete written record of your communications, as well as your thoughts and feelings between hours. If you play this game periodically in your relationship, you will not only have fun but open your intuitive powers more.

STEP *20*: *Focus on the Positive*

Since what you focus on expands, focus on the positive, but at the same time don't deny the negative. Remember to acknowledge and express gratitude towards your partner whenever you feel it. Read your SHOPPING LIST once a month and focus on seeing these qualities in your partner and acknowledging their growth. Practice forgiveness of yourself and your partner whenever necessary.

Above all, *don't* fall into the habit of complaining about your mate to friends. That's just an invitation to get more agreement—and therefore more energy—behind what you don't like. If you can't always clear your relationship *in* your relationship, if there are genuine blocks, then seek professional help to aid you. But taking complaints into your other relationships will just support the expansion of the negative.

Praise your partner to your friends. Tell them what you love, not what you hate. Share the beauty of what you and your partner are creating, and that beauty will not only grow in your life, it will serve as an inspiration to others.

STEP *21:* *The Money Game*

Play the money game together. Money is a symbol of energy in motion, God in circulation. In playing with money together you are choosing to handle more energy, aliveness, and excitement in your relationship. When you first get together, you might want to take 10% of each of your incomes and form a "common fund" to play with. You might want to open some joint accounts, for pleasure, travel, large purchases, a home. If you are not clear that each of you can support the whole relationship, build up to this certainty with a series of changing agreements.

Eventually, you will want to pool all your money together, just as you pool both your lives together, as an expression of your trust, love and devotion to each other forever. Along the way, you will notice the different ways you use money either to control and manipulate or play weak and helpless in a relationship. Out of your individual commitment to self-sufficiency, you can free yourself of the negative entanglements money used to imply.

Remember, your relationship is a business, in a sense. You handle and exchange as much money together as you do at work, at least.

So, plan together. Prepare joint goals for your future together. And if you are so moved, create a small business together—it's a way to play together more, spend more time in each other's presence, and share love and prosperity at the same time. It's doubly rewarding to do business with someone you love.

STEP *22:* *Completing The Bond*

The more you and your partner choose to be together, the more your energy fields, as well as your lives, become bonded. You may find, however, that there are subtle interferences with your bonding process that need to be purged from your subconscious minds. It is advisable, at some time in your relationship, to sit down opposite each other and share your complete sexual histories with each other—not to open a can of worms, but to share your lives completely. Sharing the past can be a great assistance to sharing the future. The process can go like this:

A: *Someone I gave my heart to in the past whom I now release forever is . . .*
B: *Thank you.*

No discussion, please! This is a simple, safe process in which to release past contracts, vows, and promises you made with others. Remember, your word is law in the universe, and if you gave your word to someone else, you must consciously withdraw that energy and put it behind your new words in order for them to be effective. You might also do meditations and visualizations in which you "see" these people from your past, complete your communications with them, and send them on their merry ways.

STEP 23: *The Marriage Game*

Never get married until you already feel married. Marriage as an expression of hope, as a promise of the future, or as a substitute for internal certainty is doomed to failure.

Marriage is an acknowledgment of a union already attained.

Of course you will continue to grow after marriage, but if there's a block before the wedding, the honeymoon won't handle it. If you're considering getting married, do the following one-to-one process until you've cleared out all limiting thoughts:

A: *A difference marriage would make is . . .*
B: *Thank you.*

Keep doing this process daily until nothing comes up. When you know marriage doesn't make a difference, you are free to get married to express the joy and harmony of your holy relationship.

STEP 24: *Support*

Couples deserve support, and there's no better means of support than surrounding yourself with other couples who are going for "having it all." The Loving Relationships Training, the Couples Training and Program are excellent support communities for conscious couples.

In the past your friendships may have been based on "misery loves company." Now it is time to surround yourself with people who support your growth, not your hopelessness. The friends that you seek are often the mirrors of the direction in which you've chosen to move.

STEP 25: *Implants For Perfect Love*

The following are additional implants to affirm the qualities you most want in a relationship. I suggest you make a cassette tape in your own voice, repeating each thought three times, pausing between each statement.

1. *I deserve unconditional love!*
2. *I deserve to receive what I want.*
3. *It's safe to surrender to people's love for me.*
4. *My love is good enough for me and everyone else.*
5. *I am a loving person.*
6. *It's safe for me to love others.*
7. *Whenever I seem to lose, a bigger win is on its way.*
8. *People love to give to me.*
9. *I now give to others the pleasure of giving to me.*
10. *I can receive without feeling obligated.*
11. *I can give without controlling others.*
12. *It pays to be giving.*
13. *I can express myself fully with others.*
14. *The more I express myself, the more I love myself.*

15. The more I express myself, the more others love me.
16. I always communicate in a way I can be heard.
17. I can create the attention I need.
18. It's safe to give myself fully.
19. I no longer hold back in my relationships.
20. The more I win, the more my partner wins.
21. The more my partner wins, the more I win.
22. I love my relationship.
23. My relationship makes my life easier.
24. I now allow my partner to support me fully.
25. I now experience support as freedom, not control.
26. I can be my full self with my partner.
27. I now allow my partner to be his full self with me.
28. I'd rather win love than arguments.
29. Since I am innocent, I no longer have to defend myself.
30. I take responsibility for what I create.
31. I can always find the solution to any problem.
32. The divine purpose of my relationship now manifests.
33. Divine guidance supports my relationship.
34. God is with us.
35. I can see the God in my partner, no matter what he is thinking, feeling or doing.
36. I now reveal my divinity to my partner.
37. It's safe to be seen fully by my partner.
38. I have nothing worth hiding from my partner.
39. My relationships always last as long as I want them.
40. It's safe to stay.
41. It's safe to leave.
42. Since I know I can leave, I'm free to stay.
43. Love is a release, not a trap.
44. The more I choose my partner, the more free I feel.
45. My primary relationship opens me up to others.
46. The more I choose my partner, the closer I feel to all my friends.
47. I no longer create separation in order to protect myself.
48. The more I surrender to my relationship, the more creativity and individuality I feel.
49. I always can see the highest thought.
50. My partner always sees the highest thought.
51. My relationship is a clear channel for inspiration.
52. I always choose pleasure over pain.
53. We deserve to have it all.

54. *It's safe to have a better relationship than my parents.*
55. *It's safe to surpass my family.*
56. *I forgive myself for having so much fun in my relationship.*
57. *I give myself permission to experience the perfection of my relationship.*
58. *My relationship is perfect, no matter what!*

My Implants for Perfect Love

_____

_____

_____

_____

_____

_____

_____

_____

_____

_____

_____

_____

_____

_____

P ♥ A ♥ R ♥ T

3

CONSCIOUS COUPLES

CONSCIOUS COUPLES

When Mallie and I first joined forces, there were no other couples around us. We felt like an island of union in the middle of a sea of single-dom. One of our first desires was to create other couples, role models we could learn from and play with. In the course of our nine years together we have succeeded in attracting some of the most magnificent relationships in the world into our lives. Many of these couples are mild-mannered, ordinary duets by day, but get them in a telephone booth, and, in a flash, they change into the super-couples they are.

Many of these couples were people we worked with in our train-ings and programs, as well as played with in our daily lives. Sometimes, it seemed impossible to know the boundaries where the friendship stopped and the teacher/student relationship began. There were days it felt we had to choose between one or the other, and that it was impossible to be friends with clients. We saw why traditional psychologists always stayed detached from their patients, and how much transference there was to deal with. But with every one of these extraordinary couples, we suc-ceeded on both levels: we learned how to put our teachings aside and relate to other couples as companions, not clients; they learned that they were our equals and that even though we had something to teach them, they were teaching us as well, and essentially we were all the same.

Mallie and I remain eternally grateful for all these people, indi-vidually and together, for all they have given us and all they have allowed us to give them. God bless you all!

Terry and Lanier

Terry and Lanier are the most inspirational couple I know. They are pioneers in the arena of human relationships—even more than Mallie and I. They are incredible friends, lovers, partners, collaborators, and companions in life. They are also extremely funny.

When I asked them what makes their relationship so extraordi-nary, Terry didn't hesitate: "Me!" he said, "My incredible tolerance for human error!''

They are both actors, comics, wonderful impersonators, and screenwriters. Their ability to play a multitude of roles without taking any of them seriously, as well as to observe the drama of other relationships from the point of view of situation comedy, lightens their relationship considerably. ''The worst things in life are the funniest things on stage!'' they say.

With most couples, the roles are clearly defined—man, woman, husband, wife, father, mother. Being two men, Terry and Lanier find their roles constantly shifting, so they never get stuck in form or fixed ways of being together. They are each willing to be each other's friend, father, mother, husband, wife, child . . . whatever is called for. One minute Terry will be a tower of strength, allowing Lanier the space to fall apart, be vulnerable, say anything, crumble. The next minute Lanier will be completely revived and Terry reduced to a puddle of tears. ''I thought you were fine,'' Lanier will say. ''I was,'' responds Terry, ''but I was just waiting for you to get it together.''

Tears turn to laughter quickly in each other's presence.

What I most admire about their relationship is that they are two human beings in love first, gay second. They don't wave banners, shout slogans, march in parades; yet they are always comfortable being who they are and sharing it in the world. When I met them in L.A., I was so amazed by their sweetness, tenderness, kindness, enthusiasm, wit, and humanity that it was only later that I realized they were in a ''gay relationship.'' Now I think of them more in a ''joyous relationship.''

Terry used to speak for the Gay Speakers Bureau, but stopped when he came to the realization that sexuality is not a political issue and all human beings share the same needs, feelings, problems, and lessons in life. He was giving a speech one day when someone asked him a dumb question, like ''What's it like to be gay?'' He looked at this person and he suddenly saw that it was all a joke, that people were asking questions they knew the answers to, and so why pretend there is separation when there's none.

Terry and Lanier have an uncanny ability to give up completely. Whenever they do, God seems to give them miracles. In fact, that's how they met. They had each just given up the hope of ever having their ideal relationship. The next day they met on a dance floor. The next evening they got all dressed up, which they never do, and went out for dinner. That was five years ago and they've been in love ever since. They also have a deep certainty that they will be together forever no matter what, which gives them great freedom to be themselves, express themselves, and tell the truth without fear of loss.

Another time they gave up completely was when their careers were stuck in L.A. Their screenplays weren't moving, their acting careers were on hold. Finally they said, "Let's forget the whole thing . . . let's move to Ojai and open a nursery." Terry crawled into bed in the fetal position. The phone rang. It was an offer from *Saturday Night Live* to write and act on the show. At first, they hesitated, knowing they didn't need the hassle of show business any more. Then they packed their bags and moved to New York.

Now Terry walks down the streets of New York and strangers— "There are no strangers," says Terry, "only people who have not yet recognized each other'—come up to him and say, "Hi . . . hello . . . how are you? . . . good show . . . enjoyed your Nancy Reagan . . ." Sometimes someone will come up and say, "Hi!" thinking he knows Terry, then suddenly realize he's a "star" and say, "Oh, it's you . . . hello!"

They've moved into their celebrity status as easily as they would into a new car. It makes no difference. For them, being stars is more a matter of how they are perceived than who they really are. And they are well aware of the American addiction to putting people on pedestals, then knocking them down.

They say the Loving Relationships Training helped them enormously. Before the training, their attitude was, "If we make it . . . if we're stars, then we'll know we're good enough!" Now they know their worth has nothing to do with external recognition, which allows them to play the show business game with less stress, more detachment, more fun. They are in love with life, themselves and each other. Everything else is a fringe benefit.

Their point of view is, in all modesty, they are God's gift to the world and the world is God's gift to them.

I tend to agree.

Peter and Meg

We first met Peter in San Francisco when he was pushing twenty years old. We noticed immediately that he was an extraordinary young man, whose heart was open and whose mind was quick. He became an instant friend. In the beginning of our relationship, Peter served us unselfishly by assisting at many of the LRTs we led in San Francisco. I think it was always our secret desire to kidnap him and bring him to New York, but we never could convince him that New York was a desirable environment.

We met Meg in New York and she signed up for our first six-month program, and has assisted and/or led at each of our subsequent programs. It was always clear that Meg was an unusually gifted human being, and that she was fully committed to her growth, relationships, and the planet. She grew up in Montana, lived in Alaska and came to the Big Apple to express herself in the world. She was a gift from God sent to us to fine tune, play with, teach, and learn from. Meg was so emotionally honest that she created the safety for hundreds of other people to surrender into.

Meg and Peter met at a Rebirthers' Convention in Colorado. Their connection was so powerful they had to go to opposite coasts and think about it for a while. We never had to match-make with them, because their purpose in being together was so strong it was inevitable they would come together. But would it be on the East Coast or the West Coast, or what about Kansas?

Meanwhile, we were trying to coax Peter to assist at our next six-month program. He was still reluctant, but there were so many clear signs that he should leave California, which he had never done in his life, that in the end he chose Meg, us, New York, and the entire East Coast. It was amazing to watch Peter once he made up his mind, how fast he moved, how totally he gave himself to his love of family in New York. Peter became one of the best LRT Trainers and Meg one of our finest Center Managers. They both succeeded individually and together in creating peace, passion and prosperity in their lives, as well as their students' lives. Now Meg is becoming a trainer and you will soon have the good fortune to be able to take LRTs with the two of them and have them tell you the story of their relationship in person.

I remember the day we married Peter and Meg. The ceremony was to be in our back yard, and both bride and groom were appropriately nervous. Peter handed me the ceremony they had written and instructed me how to do it. I started to laugh. He was organizing his own wedding as brilliantly as he would organize a seminar, training, or workshop. No wonder we say your relationship is the best training in town!

The ceremony itself was incredibly touching. Both Mallie and I felt privileged to be a part of it. We didn't really marry them, because in our hearts we never felt we had the authority to marry anyone but ourselves. But we stood there face to face with them, the mimosa tree in full blossom above us. As they spoke the vows they had chosen to make with each other, everyone in attendance surrendered to the perfection of the occasion. I know we were all thinking simultaneously, "God bless Peter and Meg!"

Robert and Doreen

When we first meet Robert and Doreen, they had been married for several years. In fact, shortly after their first LRT they decided to separate, which was not a very good omen for what eventually happened.

They lived in Queens at the time. Robert was deeply Italian and Doreen lightly Jewish. Robert's sense of humor was the first thing that grabbed us, and his ability to sing you to tears. Doreen was a fabulous dancer. She had actually won the Harvest Moon Ball Competition as a teenager, and her passion for movement predated *Flashdance*.

During their separation we got to know each of them individually, which was a real blessing. Mallie would rebirth Doreen and I would work with Robert, and sometimes the other way around. It was totally clear to us the entire nine months they were apart that they would eventually choose to be together again. We could never see them as separate. Not that we ever pushed them back together. We just waited, processed each of them, loved them unconditionally, and were not surprised when they did regroup their marriage.

The four of us became instant friends, companions, confidantes, buddies. Mallie and Doreen would go to the baths together. Robert and I would play football with the guys. It was so refreshing to Mallie and me to have "real" people in our lives, friends we didn't always have to talk enlightenment to. And even when Robert and Doreen became LRT Center Managers, and later trainers, the heart of our relationship to them remained one of friendship, beyond the circumstances of our lives at any one time.

Eventually, Robert and Doreen took the big plunge: they moved from Queens to Manhattan. In fact, they ended up living on our block, a result I had been praying for for months. We began to share our love of theater, movies, books, and sports with each other. There were times we all laughed so loud we practically collapsed. We travelled to Mexico, the Caribbean, Greece, London, and Paris together.

Robert reminded me of my dad in many ways. He was short, bald, loved movies and sports, and could take over a room by his mere presence. He was a natural leader, though it took me some time to convince him of this.

Doreen was always such a bundle of energy that she could move mountains in a breath. They were the most loving couple we had ever met. And they showed us that love can take any form. Sometimes they would fight with each other like ''the Honeymooners,'' but their devotion to the truth and their aliveness was a constant inspiration.

Once we came home from Mexico and Robert came down with spinal meningitis on his birthday. We were scared he might die. Doreen had lost her father when she was 19, and all the unresolved memories and feelings came up. When Robert recovered, we felt doubly grateful for his presence. He is truly a saint.

The next year we were in Greece on Robert's birthday. A friend of ours threw an incredible surprise party at her hotel. It was like a miracle: a feast of delectable manifestations, music, and company. It was quite a contrast to the year before.

Last year Robert's father died on Doreen's birthday. It threw our whole community into grief. Doreen got very sick and thought she was going to die. It was crazy! The shock waves sent separation, not only through Robert and Doreen's relationship, but activated all of our unconscious death urges. Their ability to go through it purged us all of our fear of death.

Mallie and I love Robert and Doreen deeply. They are living proof of what happens when the desire to surrender is greater than the fear of loss. Also, they have shown us what it means for one's life urge to be stronger than one's death urge.

Last night we ate linguini with clam sauce at Robert and Doreen's.

It was the first real time since she had been sick that Doreen had cooked for the four of us. It was so much fun. Doreen took us into their guest room and introduced their new toy: a piano. She played ''Frere Jacques'' and ''When the Saints Go Marching In'' for us.

Robert and Doreen are two divine children in one helluva divine relationship!

Gene and Helene

Gene and Helene were not immediate candidates to become our close friends. For one thing they were very much Jewish and very much from Brooklyn and reminded me too much of all my relatives who had pinched my cheeks as a child. But once we got past the stereotype we were seeing them through, we could see what a remarkable pair of people they were.

Gene and Helene had been married for twelve years when we met them. They had two beautiful children, an angel named Devin and a princess named Emily. They taught in the public school system in Brooklyn. The more I got to know them, the more I saw what brilliant teachers they were. Their love of children, patience, tolerance, wisdom, and strength was staggering. As soon as they took the LRT, they began to think of ways to incorporate these new teachings in the classroom. Then they evolved the LRT Kids' Love Shop, a one-day seminar for children nine to 16. Their results have been amazing. Parents and children all over the country are now experiencing the benefits of their gift.

I remember how Gene and Helene would drive me nuts around money. For one thing, Helene could always find the best bargain in town, even if it was out of town, and often it was in New Jersey. This obsessive bargain hunting reminded me so much of my mother that it was clear I either had to forgive my mother or kill Helene. Fortunately, I chose the former, and Gene and Helene became friends of my mother, which was clearly a match made in Brooklyn.

It was always clear to me that Gene and Helene were prosperous, but they were so disorganized about money that they never knew how much they had, where they had it, or how to get it. One minute they were broke and the next they were remembering some stock, bond, or fund with thousands of dollars in it. It became funny to watch them go through their thoughts of scarcity until they finally remembered all they had.

When they asked us to re-marry them, our first question was why? They seemed happily married already. They explained that when they conceived their marriage the first time, they were completely unconscious and just going through the motions. Now they wanted an enlightened celebration of their relationship. We agreed. The day we married them they looked so beautiful, so young, like the teenagers they were when they met. They were so much in love, it was like the first time for each of them. Mallie and I were crying. Here were these two perfect people who had had a perfectly wonderful marriage for twelve years, starting all over again, in a new spirit for a new age. When Emily appeared, she was the essence of flower girl, innocent, smiling, slowly walking down the steps, tossing rose petals around her. She moved slowly. Someone was making music. Time stopped as a child came to acknowledge her parents' union. Devin was equally precious. He looked like a Greek god come down from Olympus to bless the occasion.

Gene and Helene are two ordinary people in an extraordinary relationship. They have shared lifetimes of adventures together in this one life, not to mention the previous trips together. There is no end to their lust for life, both internally and externally. They meditate, they go to the zoo, they rebirth, they go to Coney Island, they take trainings, workshops, programs, all the while teaching full-time and loving it. Their ability to take in life and give out love is truly awesome.

When I think of Gene and Helene, I want to pinch their child-like cheeks.

Ron and Miri

Ron and Miri came to us as trained warriors. They were from Israel and had both served faithfully in the Israeli Army. They were addicted to fighting in order to survive and it was taking a toll on their relationship. Nonetheless, we all loved each other at first sight. Looking into Ron's eyes at the first LRT he did with us, I was moved to tears, hearing how his father had died when he was three months old and how he had had to grow up fast and be a father to his younger brothers. He saw his long lost father in me; I saw the brother I always wanted in him.

When we hugged it was different from other hugs. It had generations of Jewish wanderlust in its veins.

Miri was a tower of strength. She could push through anything, or resist, depending on her mood. Quite frankly, they were the most difficult couple we ever worked with, but we never felt anything but gratitude for their presence in our lives. I remember once, they were so tough I asked my mother to give them a consultation. (I had never done that before.)

Once they were assisting at an LRT. My mother was finally taking the training. I was so happy I practically forgot the other hundred people in the room and directed the whole training at her. I remember during the God section, my mother left the meeting room, and I thought she was leaving. I ran to the door, where Miri was assisting. "Where did my mom go?" I asked. "I don't know," she responded. "Well, go find her, go get her, don't let her leave, search the bathroom, do whatever it takes . . ." I was completely nuts. I wanted my mother in the room and I was blasting Miri without any justification whatsoever. Anyone but Miri might have resented me at that moment. But Miri understood. She knew me and my mother as well as I knew her and Ron. She went after my mom. A few minutes later I noticed Miri and my mom return. At the next break, I went up to Miri to apologize for my behavior. Then I asked her what had happened. "Well," she said, "I went to the bathroom like you said and I looked under every stall until I saw her feet. Then I just waited 'til she came out and came back with her." The image of Miri searching the stalls for my mother remains one of the most humorous pictures of self-improvement in my mind.

I always had this desire to lead the LRT in Israel. I somehow knew it would be important for me personally as a Jew, as well as for the world itself. As soon as I met Ron and Miri I knew God had sent them to us to bring the LRT to the Middle East. But for a long time, they were so tough, such fighters, such resisters, that I didn't know if they could do it. But they took all our programs, trainings, seminars. They, like Robert and Doreen, moved from Queens to be close to us. They were so committed to their own growth that no matter how much they fought themselves and each other, the work they were doing was taking root and producing a transformation.

When we led the first LRT in Israel in December, 1984, it was a miracle. Ron's younger brother, in the army at the time, had to check his M-16 at the hotel desk before he could enter the meeting room. There were 63 people, one big extended family, all longing for peace, love, and harmony in their lives. They sang peace songs with passion and folk songs with guts. We had Ron and Miri stand up front with us during a good part of the training and translate back and forth from Hebrew to English. They were brilliant! And when there was a tough case in the room, it didn't seem to be tough on us at all. All of a sudden I realized: Ron and Miri had been clearing us all those years we thought we were helping them, clearing us to handle the temperament of Israel once we got there. Well, it worked! The training was one of the highest experiences of my life.

Mallie and I were blown away by Ron and Miri's hospitality while we were in Israel. They drove us everywhere we wanted to go, to the Dead Sea, Masada, Jericho. They walked the streets of Jerusalem with us, took us to Bethlehem and the Church of the Holy Sepulchre. We met all their families, who took the LRT, and we felt cradled in the bosom of love in the promised land, the Holy Land. We wailed at the Wailing Wall and laughed at the walls of the City of David.

Two months later, Ron and Miri came back to New York to be on the staff of our new six-month program. At the same time, they were organizing another LRT in Tel Aviv. They were literally in two places at once, doing two successful things at once. It was amazing. At the first meeting of the program, they shared how they had been trying to have a baby without success and that their primary goal for the six months was to get pregnant. The next week Miri found out she was pregnant. It was beautiful.

All of Ron and Miri's nightmares have turned into miraculous dreams come true. They are truly a couple sent from heaven!

Larry and Joan

When Larry first appeared at an LRT, I didn't know whether I had met Chevy Chase or Humphrey Bogart. Here was this gangly, gawky guy who could make a whole room laugh without even saying anything funny, or, the next moment, brood, sulk, and sob until everyone was asking for tissues. I loved him instantly.

Larry was big and highly visible. He was obsessed with video games and his whole life was visual. Joan's personal law was *I am invisible.*

Together they made quite a team. Larry was born a month late, and his whole life seemed an effort to make up for lost time. He had grandiose schemes, big dreams he was anxious to realize, often at the expense of immediate necessities. Larry was stuck in overdrive, overkill, and overreaching. He lived in the future.

Joan didn't want to be here at all. They were worlds apart, but their love for each other was so huge it could encompass their separate planets. And they knew they had attracted each other to heal themselves: Larry, to slow down and learn how to take one step at a time; Joan, to speed up, come on out and think big.

The four of us became great friends quickly. When Larry and Joan decided to take our six-month program, we were delighted. In working with them, we learned the difficulties of working with friends, how our love for them made it more difficult to confront them when we saw something that needed shifting in them. Not that we pulled any punches. I remember once, when Larry was in the middle of his ''think too big'' phase, I gave him the assignment to shine my shoes and to get any job he could, even selling ice cream. I knew Larry had swallowed a lot of pride when he shined my shoes flawlessly and the next week got a job selling hot dogs in Battery Park. A few months later, Larry landed a high-paying position at a major New York talent agency.

We wanted to bring Joan out. We could see how wonderful she was, what a great wit, what artistic and literary talent she had. She had all the tools to express herself fully, but was too busy hiding to use them. I felt so good when she agreed to type up my first book *Open Heart Therapy.* I felt as though the book would be blessed by her innocent fingers. When Larry and Joan agreed to produce cassette tapes for Mallie and me, we formed the partnership, Open Heart Productions, which is the most pleasurable business enterprise I have ever been associated with.

When Larry and Joan asked us to marry them, we were honored. Theirs was a union totally from the heart, a union of humor and humanity that had us all laughing and crying. The wedding was a fabulous party at an old midtown restaurant. I remember there was a Jets game on TV, and all the guys ran back and forth from football to marriage. It was all loving relationships.

Most of all, I remember the day Larry and Joan's delightful baby boy, Joshua, was born. They had invited us to participate in the birth, which was to be an ''ideal birth'' at a birthing clinic on the east side. As it turned out, it was not the ''ideal'' that we had all fantasized, but the perfect birth that Joshua was choosing for himself. We spent twenty-four hours with Larry and Joan, half the time at the birthing clinic where labor kept stalling, and the other half at St. Vincent's Hospital, where a marvelous delivery team did everything possible to coax Josh out, then induce him, and, finally, when all else failed, chose, along with all of us, a perfectly wonderful cesarian solution.

They let Mallie in the delivery room to photograph the event. I walked Larry to a bar to wait. We had all cried in disappointment at the way it was turning out. Both Mallie and I were amazed to see how quickly Larry and Joan were willing to relinquish their fantasy for the will of God (and Josh) at the moment. I know we all learned more about life, surrender, struggle, faith, and perfection that day than any day of our lives. When Larry and I came back from the bar, it was 6:09 p.m. and Joshua had arrived. The nurse handed him to Larry, and there was no mistaking the father-son relationship. Josh was a baby Larry; they recognized each other instantly. He was a big boy, with a big head, too big to have pushed through Joan without hurting her. Josh had chosen the easy way out. He had known all along how he was getting here. He had just been waiting for all of us to get off our fantasies.

Our friendship with Larry and Joan has always been an open heart production!

Jane and Irv

Jane was one of my first rebirthing clients. I knew from the moment I saw her breathe that she would turn into one of the finest rebirthers in the country. She did. Jane is remarkable in her beauty, intelligence, creativity, humor, and compassion. Her commitment to her own growth was always unshakable. Her patience, persistence, and perceptiveness with her own clients makes her a tower of integrity among rebirthers.

We had always heard that Jane had this crazy husband, Irv. They were college sweethearts, who had traveled the rebellious route, lived in Mexico, beachbummed in the Caribbean. When we met them, Jane was a teacher and Irv was a rising young commercial artist working his way up the Madison Avenue ladder. We had heard all these rumors how Irv was opposed to Jane's participation in the community, how resistant he was to growth, how angry and off-the-wall he was. When we met him, we saw all this, but oh-so-much more. Irv was clearly a closet case. Behind the mask of rebel, tough guy, warrior, was a heart as soft and as sincere as they come. He was so loving, in fact, he couldn't handle it, and his brother's death and mother's insanity threw him into the closet of lost hopes and broken dreams. But his life-affirming energy remained undaunted, and the part of him that wanted to surrender was always stronger than the part of him that was frightened he would lose everything. When he would consent to get rebirthed, he would be an instant puddle of tears. He had such a great sense of humor to disguise his pain, but it was always there, beneath the surface, crying out for help. He would give us double messages all the time, on the one hand telling us to keep away from him, and, on the other, crying out not to be left. We loved him so much and so unconditionally it never made a difference to us what mood he was in. We felt blessed by his presence. When he took the LRT and shared his feelings, a hundred people cried in unison.

Jane became a leader in the community. Irv became a successful Art Director on Madison Avenue. I remember when he started working on an Army account. He had created the perfect job to express the fighter part of himself. Jane was teaching peace with passion in all her seminars and consultations. They were both teaching each other, Jane learning that it was safe to assert herself more fully and that men would not hurt her, Irv learning that the battlefield was really in his own mind and that he could survive without conflict. Recently, Irv gave up the Army account for a cheese account. We all smiled.

Jane was the first one in the community to get pregnant. She was so petite that it was funny to see her get so big. They invited us to attend the birth, and we were excited by the prospect. But our schedule was so busy that the only way we could be in attendance was if the baby decided to come between trips to New Mexico and Greece. The day we were leaving for Greece we sensed it was going to happen. But our plane left before Jesse came. *C'est la vie.*

Jesse is the little prince of our community. Jane has been an infinite reservoir of nurturing, patience, and love. To see Irv with his son would bring tears to anyone's eye. They dance to Bruce Springsteen and watch MTV in tandem. Irv, Jane, and Jesse: an extraordinary family unit! A pocket of love you can always count on!

I would like to acknowledge the following other couples for their love, devotion and contribution to the family of loving relationships:

Scott and Suzanne	*Hans and Christie*
Rocky and Prudence	*Jeremy and Carol*
Patrick and Kaye	*Diane and Ronnie*
Steven and Trina	*Bonnie and David*
Steve and Marsha	*Jim and Pru*
Tommy and Linda	*Michael and Ila*
Charlie and Mary Jane	*Philip and Mikela*
Wayne and Katrina	*David and Doreen*
Vincent and Yvonne	*Ken and Maureen*
Alex and Gayle	

And to my very dear friends, George and Carol.

ABOUT THE AUTHOR

Bob Mandel is the author of *Open Heart Therapy* (published by Celestial Arts, 1984) and is the National Director of the Loving Relationships Training. He is a Certified Rebirther and consultant. In 1980 he founded the International Seminars Leadership Programs (ISLP) which trains individuals to break through to their leadership potential. He holds advanced degrees from Columbia and has been involved with the Yale School of Drama, The New Theatre of London, and the Theatre Arts Corporation of New Mexico. This is his second book.

Professional Rebirthers

I heartily recommend the following Rebirthers:

New York

Peter and Meg Kane
34 West 85th Street, Apt. 1
NYC, NY 10024
(212) 580-8031

Robert & Doreen Marine
34 West 87th Street
NYC, NY 10024
(212) 877-7003

Judy Roberts
114 West 76th Street #BR
NYC, NY 10024
(212) 362-0083

Jane Klein
119 Payson Avenue
NYC, NY 10034
(212) 569-8598

Wendy McLeod
125 West 85th Street
NYC, NY 10024
(212) 724-3652

Suzanne Browner
254 West 98th Street #2B
NYC, NY 10025
(212) 316-0013

Judy Roberts
418 Central Park W. #103
NYC, NY 10025
(212) 662-9768

Ron & Miri Gilad
342 W. 85th St. #3D
NYC, NY 10024
(212) 595-1369

David & Bonnie Hampton
227 Central Park W. #3D
NYC, NY 10024
(212) 787-1327

Marsha Mowery
93 Bedford St. #3C
NYC, NY 10014
(212) 675-6515

Cathy Baggaley
164 E. 78th Street
NYC, NY 10021
(212) 772-9359

Massachusetts

Jose & Nice Santiago
P.O. Box 2627
Cambridge, MA 02238
(617) 864-0373

Pennsylvania

Anthony LoMastro
2431 Brown Street
Philadelphia, PA 19130
(215) 765-7958

Karen Crenziger
4819 Osage Ave.
Philadelphia, PA 19143
(215) 474-2527

Ohio

Karen Trennepohl
5074 Western Hills Ave.
Cincinnati, Ohio 45238
(513) 471-2410

Charles & Mary Jane Hostick
8292 Miami Road
Cincinnati, Ohio 45243
(513) 891-0559

Washington, D.C.

Michael & Ila Shapiro
205 Yoakum Parkway #1504
Alexandria, VA 22304
(703) 370-1963

Emily Goldman
2226 River Road N.W.
Washington, D.C. 20016
(202) 362-5162

Laura Harrison
8801 Maywood Avenue
Silver Spring, MD 20910
(301) 587-8237

Jim and Bev Worseley
1650 Moorings Dr. #22C
Reston, VA 22090
(703) 471-0247

Georgia

Jim & Pru Collier
202 Ansley Villa Drive
Atlanta, GA 30324
(202) 872-9570

Patrick & Gay Golan
203 Ansley Villa Drive
Atlanta, GA 30324
(404) 875-2616

Kay Sessions
P.O. Box 3013
Atlanta, GA 30301
(404) 221-5735 (work)

Florida

Mikela Green
P.O. Box 537
N. Miami Beach, FL 33160
(305) 279-5882

Philip Tarlow
1173 South A1A
Hillsboro Beach, FL 33062
(305) 426-3902

Texas

Madeline Schaider
1407 Missouri, Suite 101
Houston, TX 77006
(713) 523-6419

Elen Caldwell
3809 N. Braeswood #4
Houston, Texas 77006
(713) 668-4225

Colorado

Kate Lessley
1320 Steele Street
Denver, CO 80206
(303) 388-8820

Katy Stubbs
1187 Elm
Denver, CO 80220
(303) 320-5302

California

Ken & Maureen Richards
1430 43rd Avenue
San Francisco, CA 94122
(415) 759-7575

Bobby Birdsall
7810 Laurel Canyon #6
Los Angeles, CA 90065
(818) 765-2410

Phil Laut
1636 N. Curson Avenue
Hollywood, CA 90046
(213) 876-6226

Linda Priest
13803 Valley Vista Blvd.
Sherman Oaks, CA 91423
(818) 995-6579

Eve Jones
140 S. Norton
Los Angeles, CA 90004
(213) 461-5774

Rhonda Levand
1251 Fairburn Avenue
Los Angeles, CA 90024
(213) 470-4501

Manny Stamatakis
3406 Glendon Avenue #8
Los Angeles, CA 90034
(213) 202-0499

Leonard Orr
Campbell Hot Springs
P.O. Box 234
Sierraville, CA 96126
(916) 994-8984

Joe Moriarty
Campbell Hot Springs
P.O. Box 234
Sierraville, CA 96126
(916) 994-8984

Jeanne Jones
842 S. Wooster
Los Angeles, CA 90035
(213) 854-0770

Washington State

David & Doreen Tannenbaum
P.O. Box 22704
Seattle, WA 98122
(206) 236-0228

Hawaii

Alex Lukeman
Gayle Carlton
P.O. Box 811
Hanalei, Kauai
Hawaii 96714
(808) 826-6924

Genora Woodruff
5296 A Haleilio Rd.
Kapaa, Hawaii 96746
(808) 822-1726

Europe

Gillian Steel
Colne Denton
Old Ferry Wharf
Cheyne Walk
London SW10 England
D11 441 352 3977

Diana Roberts
9d Claverton Street
London SW1
01 630 1501

Ben Bartle
143 Willifield Way
London, NW116XY
01-455-4043

Richard Bachard
15 Rue de Fontarabie
Bte 86
75020 Paris, France
367-6411

Marianne Thorsell
Krukmakaragtan 18
Stockholm 11651 Sweden
08848616

Australia

Yvonne & Vincent Betar
44 Rae Street
Fitzroy North, Victoria 3068
Australia
61-3-481-5302

Wayne & Katrina O'Donovan
G.P.O. Box 950
Sydney, N.S.W. 2001
Australia

OTHER PRODUCTS BY BOB & MALLIE MANDEL:

Cassette Tapes & Books

Money Mantras (the tape). A 60-minute meditation of prosperity affirmations designed to open you up to receive greater abundance in all areas of your life.

Money Mantras (the book). A 30-day course designed to strengthen your connection to God, thereby increasing your capacity to manifest money miracles.

Amazing You! A self-esteem tape featuring affirmations, visualizations, and music designed to support you in loving yourself unconditionally and attracting your ideal partner.

Having It All! An audio-musical on tape designed to magnetize you to attract your ideal body, home, car, friends, relationships, and sex life.

Peace With Passion! A fabulous musical odyssey on tape, consisting of affirmations, visualizations, gospel and rock music, designed to release all conflict from your mind, body, spirit, relationships, and the planet.

To order cassette tapes, send $12 each (postpaid) to:

Open Heart Productions
424 Forest Avenue
New Rochelle, NY 10804

Or call Open Heart Productions for more information at (914) 633-3110. If ordering more than five tapes, call or write for discount information.

For further information on Bob and Mallie's long-term programs, *Create-A-Mate*, the Loving Relationships Training, and related seminars, contact:

Guided Productions
145 West 87th Street
New York, NY 10024
or
(212) 799-7323

You can also call these numbers for information about Rebirthing.

A WORD FROM THE PUBLISHER

Celestial Arts is the publisher of many excellent books on personal growth, health, and wellness, with an emphasis on topics of awareness such as rebirthing, meditation, consciousness, and miracles.

Among our bestselling authors are Sondra Ray—founder of the *Loving Relationships Training* and author of *Drinking the Divine, I Deserve Love, Celebration of Breath, The Only Diet There Is, Ideal Birth, and Rebirthing in the New Age.*

We also publish Virginia Satir, Richard Moss, Barry Stevens, Jerry Jampolsky, Kenneth R. Pelletier, Alan Watts, Emmett E. Miller, and Elson M. Haas.

We also publish children's books and a complete line of posters and graphics.

For a copy of our free catalog, write or call: Celestial Arts, P.O. Box 7327, Berkeley, CA 94707 (415) 524-1801.

A WORD FROM TEN SPEED PRESS

In 1983 *Celestial Arts* became a part of *Ten Speed Press,* publishers of career and life guidance books including *What Color Is Your Parachute?,* and other books on bicycling, outdoors, and cookbooks. Please write or call for their free catalog: Ten Speed Press, P.O. Box 7123, Berkeley, CA 94707 (415) 845-8414.

Life is more than something to endure! Life is more than survival! If you were to stop and think about it, you would have to acknowledge that your life is the greatest gift in the world—a possession so precious you would not give it up for all the money in the world. Yet how often do you fully appreciate the simple but incredible miracle of being alive?

It is never too late to start over. You can still recover your lost innocence, renew your faith, and harness your creative energy to build a richer life for yourself and others. You can recapture the romance of your youth, awaken your mind to new excitement, and release the numbness from your body.

You are never too old to be young at heart!

Open Heart Therapy could very well be the answer to all those dreams you may have almost given up believing in!

OPEN HEART THERAPY
by Bob Mandel

Price: $7.95
Pages: 160
Size: 7¼ x 8½

Available from Celestial Arts, P.O. Box 7327, Berkeley, CA 94707 (415) 524-1801. Please include $1.00 for postage and handling via U.S. fourth class bookpost or $2.25 extra for UPS shipping and handling. *California residents only:* please add 6.5% sales tax (52 cents per book).